THE CONFIDENTIAL FILES
OF
MICHAEL JACKSON

UNAUTHORIZED and UNCENSORED

Damian Iwueke

Published by New Generation Publishing in 2016

Copyright © Damian Iwueke 2016

First Edition

The author asserts the moral right under the Copyright, Designs and Patents Act 1988 to be identified as the author of this work.

All Rights reserved. No part of this publication may be reproduced, stored in a retrieval system or transmitted, in any form or by any means without the prior consent of the author, nor be otherwise circulated in any form of binding or cover other than that which it is published and without a similar condition being imposed on the subsequent purchaser.

www.newgeneration-publishing.com

CHAPTERS

MICHAEL JACKSON DIES..........................	1
A STAR IS BORN.......................................	12
JACKSON 5-*Emergence of an icon*.................	25
KING OF POP..	38
THE PRICE OF STARDOM..........................	46
MICHAEL JACKSON Vs THE MEDIA- *How tabloids survive on blackmail and extortion*..	51
MICHAEL JACKSON AND WOMEN	74
MICHAEL JACKSON AND OPRAH WINFREY...	101
MICHAEL JACKSON Vs MARTIN BASHIR...	103
THE DAMAGE OF LA TOYA JACKSON......	111
PAEDOPHILE OR MISUNDERSTOOD...	118
THIS IS IT-*Fall of an icon*......................	123

DISCLAIMER

Many well known people including President Barack Obama, organizations, newspapers and magazines are mentioned in this book. The author wishes to stress that no disrespect is meant to the individuals and organizations mentioned herein. Neither does the book apportion blame to the individuals or organizations mentioned herein as being responsible for the death of Michael Jackson. The book is an in-depth analysis of Michael Jackson's relation with the media and the reasons why he got engaged in the self-destructive habit of taking anaesthetic and powerful drugs which eventually killed him.

The book has nothing to do with conspiracy theories about the death of Michael Jackson including those from his sister LaToya which have been circulating in the mainstream and social media.

The book is based on reliable information which has been gathered from sources close to Michael Jackson over a period of five years since his death on 25 June 2009.

DAMIAN IWUEKE

PREFACE

Michael J. Jackson was an artist and an entertainer of incomparable talent. Although many of us viewed him as elusive, mysterious, eccentric and complex but to those who knew him best he was a simple and kind-hearted man. At the peak of his career, the late King of Pop's global popularity surpassed that of Coca-Cola and computer. Unfortunately he spent half of his adult life struggling to evade intrusion of the media and gold diggers who were bent on exploiting him. His troubles were overwhelming and he could not find place to hide. At one point he was the richest entertainer in the world but ended up dying with a struggle to support himself and his three children. He degenerated into using powerful and anti-depressant drugs which eventually led to his tragic death on 25 June 2009.

Through personal interviews with people who knew Michael very well, Damian has been able to uncover a new side of the man whom many of us considered 'strange' and 'mysterious'. Michael Jackson was a man whose life was a 'thriller' just like his music; he was also a person who fascinated the public until the very end. This uncensored book takes a deep look at the life of the man you never knew, his relationship with the world and in particular with the media. Michael Jackson was a musician whom the author was very passionate about and this book is a posthumous legacy in his honour.

It is my pleasure therefore to present to Michael Jackson's fans and to the public in general, this fascinating memoir of the late King of Pop.

Janice Warford
Kessingland; Suffolk, England

ACKNOWLEDGMENTS

In the course of writing any biography, whether authorized or unauthorized as in the case of this book, a tremendous amount of research is necessary. I drew upon many sources in the lengthy process of compiling this book including interviewing a number of people who were close to Michael Jackson and who knew his non-celebrity persona. Other people who knew the Jacksons way back in Gary, Indiana and later in California also spoke to me. Many aspects of the singer's life which until now has not been made public, are divulged in this book. Some people who were very close to Michael and spoke to me in confidence have asked me not to mention them by name; I am respecting their wishes. While those sources cannot be listed, I am very grateful to each one of them for talking to me and for supporting my endeavour.

A lot of articles including books have been written and published about Michael Jackson, however, writing a book based on his 'thoughts' and information received from very reliable sources close to him and the Jackson family was not an easy task. Due to the complexities involved in writing an unauthorized biography of a superstar of his stature, it has taken more than five years to complete this book. To gather the information that was necessary for this memoir, I had to reach out to many sources from across the world. The project itself could not have been possible without the support, help and encouragement of some family members and friends.

First and foremost, my thanks and gratitude goes to my son Julien who painstakingly typed the manuscript over three summers. While on holiday from college, Julien stayed home most of the summer of 2010, 2011 and 2012 to click away on his computer in order to make sure that the manuscript was delivered to me well before the final submission date I had given him. There were also other members of the family who contributed towards ensuring that the project is completed, they include the mother of my children, Graziella and my daughter Kristina.

In Malta, England, Bulgaria, USA and Nigeria:

I am very grateful to Franco Portelli-one of Malta's best literary agents - who gave me advice on the best way to go about publishing the book. I also owe a lot of gratitude to Dr Nnamdi Ahunanya and his wife Comfort, Rev. Fr. Adrian Cachia, Richard and Doris Matrenza, Dr Leslie Cushieri, Dr James Calleja and Prof Salvino Busuttil, all who supported me in different ways respectively when I first arrived in Malta. Without these people mentioned above, I may not have become who I am today and be in a position to write this book.

In England, I would like to thank my friends Janice Warford, Joe Onwukwem, Pastor Bright Iwo and Joe Formosa and his family in Blackpool for the assistance which the latter especially, offered me during my stay in the English seaside town from where I started writing this book in October 2009. I am grateful to Olga Savinska (Ukraine), Sladjana Spaic (USA) and Denitsa Bankova (Bulgaria) all of whom have also contributed in different ways to make sure that this project was completed.

My special gratitude goes to Janice Warford for her personal and professional support which is immeasurable. Janice was there for me from the start of the project, right to the end.

My heart goes out to Donna McCartney of Ebook Empress, Virginia, USA, who suggested the initial title and cover photo for this book but which have been substituted with the present one. When I was in contact with Donna, I had some doubts whether I should continue with the project but she asked me not to loose hope and encouraged me to continue writing the book. After going through the synopsis which I sent her, she said that she was of the opinion that the book is different from many others that have been written about Michael Jackson.

My heart go out to my sisters Adanne Ndubuka, Cyrina Iwueke, Anne Ndu, Mary Awokoya, Juliana Agulehi and my niece Chika Nnanna who have all been very supportive of the endeavour. I am grateful to my former high school Principal Mr J.A. Garrod from Newmarket, England who suggested and encouraged me to study Librarianship, Economics and International Relations at the university, a career path which has helped me to develop as a writer.

Some of the quotations included in this work have been culled from the list of publications which are listed in the last page of this book. I acknowledge and I am very grateful and thankful for the sources mentioned therewith.

Thank you to my editors Lucienne Cassar and Janice Warford both of whom respectively and painstakingly polished the manuscript to make it ready for publication. While I bear full responsibility for the contents of this book, Lucienne and Janice turned my manuscript into a book which I hope will contribute towards preserving the memory of Michael Jackson.

DAMIAN IWUEKE
Watford, United Kingdom
June, 2016

DEDICATED TO THEIR MEMORIES

DO NOT FORGET THE KING OF POP

Michael Jackson *29 August 1958-25 June 2009*
"No one knows who I am. No one knows the truth. And the longer it takes them to know, to discover me, the more famous I will be" -***Michael Jackson***

Bob Marley *1945-1981*

"Emancipate yourself from mental slavery"-***BobMarley***

Fela Anikulapo Kuti *1938-1995*

*"Teacher, don't teach me nonsense"-**Fela***

Tupac Amaru Shakur *1971-1996*

*"Every body is at war with different things. I'm at war with my heart"-**Tupac***

DEDICATED ALSO

To Joseph and Katherine Jackson without whom there will be no Jackson 5 and the King of Pop Michael Jackson.

To my late parents Dennis and Theresa Iwueke who sent me off to university but were both passed by the time I graduated.

CHAPTER ONE

MICHAEL JACKSON DIES

"Michael, now that you have gone, may be they will leave you alone."

- **Marlon Jackson**

25th June 2009, was a day that shocked me. I was getting ready for bed at about 22.45hrs, when I chanced a glimpse towards my television, which I normally leave muted, and saw photos of Michael Jackson splashed across the screen accompanied by a *Breaking News* caption. Two things flashed through my mind as the possible source of this news: which venue was Michael going to perform at next; what has he been accused of now?

As I raised the volume and sat down to listen, my heartbeat increased as I became more frantic. The initial news was that Michael Jackson had been rushed to hospital in a coma. This was followed by other news segments, each one providing additional information. Updates about him were continuously broadcast on all major networks worldwide. For the first few hours however, the news was conflicting. There was no way I would sleep and risk missing what I thought was some important news about Michael Jackson.

Then after one or two hours, there was the bombshell! *Breaking News* flashed on my TV screen 'Michael Jackson dies'! The time was about 12.15am local time in Britain! As I zapped between *BBC* and various other news channels in the early hours of the 25th June (UK time), my whole body began to shake. I started sweating, trying to convince myself that this could not possibly be true. I was glued to the TV but was actually seeing nothing! Michael Jackson dead? No, no way. As the thoughts flowed through my brain, so were tears streaming down my cheeks. The only two persons I have ever shed tears in my life for, are my mother when she passed away and Michael

Jackson. Yes, I did cry for the death of Michael Jackson!

So after getting through the death of one of the greatest entertainers the world has ever seen, in October 2009, I began putting plans together to write this memoir in his honour. So this book explores how Michael Jackson, though a very happy person when he was young, with young friends, his children and pets and when writing songs and working or rehearsing in his private studio, would later in life become a different person-withdrawn from every thing life has to offer-becaus he was trying to avoid the constant harassment of the establishment, the media organizations and gold diggers.

He may have physically died in June 2009 but the real Michael Jackson we all knew way back from the 1960s, was already a dead man walking from 2003 when he was accused for the second time of molesting another teenager called Garvin Avizo. That including the first 1993 accusation by Jody Chandler's family, backed by the media who wanted to increase sales of their papers and TV viewership, became a big burden which Michael had to live with for the rest of his life. Michael Jackson did quash the first accusation by paying a heavy ransom to the Chandler family, but the damage to his reputation had already been done and was compounded when he was charged for the second offence. So from 1993 to the day he eventually died in 2009, he never was quite able to remove the stain which the two scandals caused him and his image as a respected pop star. After paying big to get free from prosecution for the Chandler accusation in 1993, Michael foolishly continued befriending young boys and, without realising the further damage he was bringing upon his image, including indirectly digging his own grave, ten years after the Jody Chandler saga, he gave permission to Martin Bashir to film him in an awkward position in the company of one of the young boys who were staying at his home. Allowing Martin Bashir to enjoy all the privileges available at his home and travel all over America and the the rest of the world with him in order to film and produce the documentary *Living with Michael Jackson* was a terrible error of judgement which equated to signing his death warrant. So while Michael Jackson dug himself into a grave with that lapse of judgement, Bashir used the unsuspecting superstar to raise his journalistic profile.

Just like Bashir, other people who used or framed Michael Jackson for their personal gain, should search their conscience and reflect whether they directly or indirectly contributed to his unhappiness which eventually culminated to his sudden death. Reliable sources close to Michael told me that between 1993 and 2007, he paid out close to $300 million dollars to people from different walks of life who framed him for one 'crime' or the other, most of which I have been informed related to child abuse and even pregnancy claim from ladies who said they were carrying Michael Jackson's child. Sources close to Michael say that from 2004-2007 they witnessed almost every 6 months, cheques of between $10-50 million been paid out by Jackson to settle legal cases, most of them relating to child molestation accusations that were flying in from all angle. They said that Michael chose to settle the cases, not because he committed the crimes but for the simple reason that he wanted people to leave him alone. After Jody Chandler and Gavin Arvizo cases, Michael became very angry, exhausted and depressed. It transpired that while he was paying out a lot of money to lawyers and to people who had sued him, Michael was running out of money. In the meantime, his domestic and security staff were not paid their wages for several months. However, irrespective of the difficult financial situation that was developing around him, the people working for him continued to perform their duties out of the love they had for him and his children, while hoping and believing that their boss Michael Jackson, with his unquestionable talent, would bounce back and start making money once again. According to one of them, who spoke to me on condition of anonymity, the staff members who remained with Michael were quite aware that he was not guilty of the accusations which some individuals and the police accused him of committing. They also believed that the problems which led to their delayed wages were due to greedy people and gold diggers who were doing everything possible to extort money from Michael. My sources thought that the singer and his advisers could have done better instead of capitulating to ransom demands: *"It was not right that they were ever eager to write out cheques to keep things quiet instead of examining properly why Michael was receiving compensation demands."*

Michael Jackson paid a tremendous price for entertaining us. The curse of his fame and wealth caught up with him. This was not what he wanted. But such is the irony of success as it opens one up for scrutiny and exploitation. Michael Jackson was a mega star so the media and many gold diggers were bent on exploiting him. Those who directly or indirectly feasted on Michael Jackson included individuals, media organizations, corporations, the paparazzis and some members of his family. As to his family, he once commented: *"You see what they do to me? I have supported them all. But still they come after me for more."* Michael Jackson no doubt loved his fans but he would also go to great lengths to avoid people because he was overwhelmed by various types of demands from different people and organizations. From the mid 1908s until his death in 2009, half of Michael's private time was spent trying to avoid people and media organizations who wanted to use his name and or his image to make money. He would often disguise himself before leaving his house or hotel and it was also impossible for him to hold down any real friendships or romantic relationship for that matter. He also regularly changed his telephone numbers so that even some members of his family could not reach him.

As Michael Jackson became very successful and was making lot of money so did his personal troubles increase and he suddenly realised that he has a lot on his shoulders. When he was in Jackson 5 with his brothers he was the major factor in the income they made as a unit. But from the age of 5 until his death at 50, Michael was not really and fully at peace with himself. Then the last 20 years of his life became the worst in many respects as he was burdened with two accusations of child abuse, including the media literally chasing him every day of his life. He ended up beign angry, confused and paranoid. Although the world was his stage and we were his fans, his desire was to interact with us only on that stage and after wards retire to his own private world and be left alone. He was, however, confused on how to go about it. So, to make his escape a reality, he chose to bcome elusive. Meanwhile, as he locked himself up in his *Neverland* home and later in the mansion he rented in downtown California shortly before died, he suffered insomnia and was paranoid. Eating properly became a problem and his health began to take a turn for the worst. As Michael had no 'true' friend and had reduced or cut off contact with his immediate family, he had no one to turn to for support. Instead he turned to anti-depressant drugs, which in the end claimed his life.

Dr Conrad Murray, who arrived on the scene in later years, was merely the symptom and not the cause of Michael's troubles and subsequent death. Any suggestion or claim that Dr Murray was chiefly responsible for the death of Michael Jackson is nonsense. And for him to have been jailed for the death of the singer was a miscarriage of justice. Dr Conrad Murray was a scape goat. It happened to be that he was in a wrong place at the wrong time and became the fall guy. After Michael's death, the white media influenced public opinion against Dr Murray and played a crucial role in the jury's decision to convict him for the involuntary manslaughter of Michael Jackson. Blaming Murray for Michael Jackson's death was good for the media because it exonerated them from the troubles they gave Michael Jackson, part of which was the reason he locked himself up, became very depressed and degenerated into drugs which killed him. Even while still on his death bed, the media, especially the tabloids still went into over drive to continue to publish sensational stories about the dead singer and the professional relationship he had with his doctor. The media were not concerned about the fate of Michael Jackson who was still on his death bed rather their main aim was to increase the circulation and sale of their newspapers.

Michael Jackson may have been a superstar for his fans, but in the eyes of the media he was simply a money-making machine. The extent to which the tabloids twisted articles of the life and death of Michael Jackson shows how some journalists can spin the stories they feed the public. Most times journalists don't care about the truth and the facts as long as the reading public are held in suspense. Tabloids make readers buy and imbibe their own version of any story. The moral part of what of tabloids do is not important to them as long as the money rolls in. Michael Jackson could not control, influence or stop the negative things the press were writing about him.

Irrespective of what has been said above as regards Dr Conrad Murray, I believe that the doctor failed Michael Jackson though. As a medical practioner with long experience, he was aware that his patient was addicted to anti-depressant drugs and was at risk, yet he continued to administer him with a mixture of powerful Propofol and Demerol drugs. Dr Murray did not alert the Jackson family in the strongest way possible or the AEG for that matter who had signed the singer to perform in London in July 2009 before he suddenly died one month earlier. He probably didn't do so because he didn't want to loose the contract of beign Michael's private doctor which would have prevented him from earning more money if Michael had carried out the London concerts as planned. It seems then that Conrad Murray was only interested in making money from the singer and AEG and shied away from his responsibilty. Murray has recently written a silly book with no facts at all except to make money once again from Jackson's name by describing how he and the singer used the services of strippers, prostitutes and escorts whenever they travelled out of town. Shortly before the publication of this book, I quickly contacted my sources in America who are close to Michael Jackson and they told me that what Conrad Murray has written about Michael using escorts is COMPLETE LIE, FABRICATION and NONSENSE! They said that they are not surprised then that he was jailed for the involuntary manslaughter of Michael Jackson. He is a hypocrite, they said!

In the course of writing this book, I read and listened to many people, including some of the people who were close to Michael. One thing they all agreed is that Michael hated the tabloid press when he was alive. They said Michael was given a tremendously difficult time by the tabloids and mainstream press, as well as the police and gold diggers. The print press in particular, in their pursuit for newspaper sales, pushed and probed so much so that they ended up making Michael Jackson extremely an unhappy man. Those close to Michael also said that it was like the establishment in America and their media organizations could not stand a black man who was successful and famous. The American media establishment pretended that they loved Michael Jackson when in reality they loathed him.

Enter the British press. Of all the scornful, negative and damaging stories that were written about Michael Jackson, no tabloids did it more than the three owned by Rupert Murdoch. The brash *News of the World* which has been closed down because of its criminal activities and replaced with *The Sun on Sunday* and their daily sister paper *The Sun* lampooned Michael Jackson so much so that they could win award for all the negative stories they published about him. In order to compete with Murdoch's tabloids, other British tabloids including the *Daily Star* and the *Mirror* also joined the fray to continuously bash Michael Jackson. The English tabloids were successful in increasing their circulation and sale of their newspapers whenever they publish stories concerning Michael Jackson because they were feeding the British peoples' hunger for gossip and sensationalism. Michael Jackson was a mega star, he was also well-loved in Britain therefore, any story about him whether true or false was bound to sale and the country's tabloids exploited this fact. Because of the love of the singer in Britain, the British press became more fascinated about him than their American counterparts.

Reliable sources informed me that Michael used to follow what the the British press were writing about him but when he realised that most of the things they published were false and fabrications, he decided to ignore them. He thought about taking legal action in some cases but he also knew that it would give more publicity to the tabloids. Although some of the stories did hurt Michael and his family but at the same time they would laugh them off and move on. Because Michael Jackson was the biggest star on the planet in those days, the British and the American media had a field day stalking and harassing him. At his memorial service on July 12, 2009 at the Staple Centre in California, his brother, Marlon reminded the media that the game was over when he knelt in front of his brother's casket and said *"Michael, now that you have gone, may be they will leave you alone."*

Since Michael's death in 2009, the table has turned for the British tabloid newspapers. One of them *News of the World* was found out for the fraud it was and has since been shut down. Among other things, the newspaper was found to be engaging in criminal activities to obtain some of the news and exclusive stories they were dishing out to the public. As the newspaper was folding up, some of the journalists who perpetrated the crime of stealing and tapping private individual's telephone systems were jailed. However, the lady who was incharge and presided over some of the stories that were stolen from the illegal tapping of individuals' telephones was absolved from blame and went scot free.

In the meantime, Rupert Murdoch, owner of *News of the World* who has made millions from selling exclusive stories many of which were stolen from peoples' mobile telephones has rebranded the defunct *News of the World* and it is now called *Sun on Sunday.*

The day Michael Jackson died, news of his death spread like wildfire.The internet rush to find out what actually happened to him caused many websites to crash. The American gossip website *TMZ* and *Los Angeles Times* both of which broke the news of his death suffered outages in their websites. Google and Yahoo websites were also affected. Michael Jackson's death triggered an outpouring of grief from millions of people from all over the world. While Jackson's fans were shocked and grieving, the media who demonised him during most of his adult life dived into another round of frenzy because to them Jackson's death had brought a new opportunity for yet more sensational news in order increase circulation and sell papers.The print media aside, the death of Michael Jackson generated Amazon online music shop millions of dollars in sales. Sale of Michael Jackson's CD in the week he died doubled more than the company ever sold of his music in the 11 years Amazon was established before 2009. Since his death, Michael Jackson's Estate has earned more than $500 million from sale of his music and videos and the figure continues to rise to this day.

Michael Jackson's death was covered 24/7 by the news media from all over the world. His death could also be described as 'good news' in disguise for newspapers, paparazzis, television and radio stations because each of these media organizations increased the circulation of their papers, TV viewership and consequently benefited from more advertisement which came in the wake of the news of his death. Any news about Michael Jackson in life or in death and whether true or fabricated, were still of interest to the public so the media capitalised on the opportunity and continued serializing on Michael Jackson's stories. In England during the week Michael died, circulation and sale of *News of the World* and her sister tabloid *The Sun* including those of their competetors *Daily Star and Mirror* doubled to thousands more than they were used to before his death.

As the English tabloids witnessed a rise in their circulation during Jackson's death, they raised the tempo further with such headlines as: ***"Wacky Family", "Wacko Jacko", "Jacko Stacko", "Jack from the Dead"*** and ***"Wake-O Jacko"*** among others. In other to outwit each other with attention grabbing headlines, the dead singer was demonised and humiliated in various articles that were written about him. The press people didn't care about his death or the pain his family was going through, their main concern was to sell more newspapers.

Michael Jackson was the best known black man that ever lived. His world wide fame despite some missteps along the way dwarfs that of Martin Luther King, Nelson Mandela, Barack Obama, Pele, Mohammed Ali, Michael Jordan and Tiger Woods among other great black men. The white media might have had an agenda against Michael Jackson but some black brothers were also jealous of him. When Michael died on 25 June 2009, President Barack Obama, the first black President of the United States made no comments about his death until 24 hours later. There was also no official statement from the White House either. It was only when a journalist from the AP news agency confronted Obama about Jackson's death that the President issued what appeared to be a scripted answer. Even so, the President was rather cold in his comment. In what seemed like appeasing to the white establishment, he made a rather derogatory remark in which he insinuated that the life Michael Jackson lived was a pity. And from the president's body language in front of the interviewer's camera, he looked uncomfortable mentioning Michael's name. Perhaps the president didn't like the fact that Michael Jackson before he died was more popular than him. While President Ronald Reagan and Bill Clinton at various times hosted Michael Jackson at the White House, Obama did not see the need to pay tribute to a fellow great black American who passed away.

In comparison, Obama's reactions respectively in April and June 2016 when the musician Prince and Mohammed Ali died were remarkably different as was his handling of the death of a certain Michael Brown in August 2014. Michael Brown of Ferguson, Missouri who was described as a petty thief by the store owner where he went to buy some cigarettes was shot dead after a scuffle with the police. His death led to some public protests in his community. Questions were raised about his character but the President for political correctness felt the need to send a representative from the White House to Mr Brown's funeral. But the President ignored Michael Jackson's death and his funeral service. Jackson might have been accused of child abuse but he was never found guilty or convicted of any of the charges. The President is a lawyer and knows that a person is presumed innocent until proven guilty. But while Michael Jackson was a megastar who was a rival to Obama in status, Michael Brown from Ferguson who was no match to the President and was said to be a petty criminal attracted the attention of the President just for political correctness.

While Obama did not feel the need to honour Michael Jackson, other world and business leaders did. Among them the late Nelson Mandela of South Africa, former British Prime Minister Gordon Brown and Mohammed Fayed, the Egyptian born-British millionaire and former owner of the Harrods Store in London, all paid tribute to Michael Jackson. Mohammed Fayed went as far as erecting a statue as a tribute to the late King of Pop at the Fulham Football stadium in London. He also included a memorial corner at Harrods featuring Michael Jackson. The British Prime Minister Gordon Brown released a statement from Downing Street in which he said:*"This is very sad news for the millions of Michael Jackson fans in Britain and around the world. The British peoples' thoughts are with Michael Jackson's family at this time."*

CHAPTER TWO

A STAR IS BORN

"Jackson 5 was born out of a tradition"
-Michael Jackson

Michael Jackson was born on August 29th 1958, in Gary, Indiana, USA. He was the seventh child of nine born to Joseph and Katherine Jackson. At the age of five Michael was already singing and performing with his elder brothers Jackie, Tito, Jermaine and Marlon.

Their father, Joseph Jackson, was a steel mill worker and part-time musician. The family had music in their genes as Joseph's parents were also part-time musicians. Joseph Jackson formed a local band called the Falcons and the group practiced at the Jackson's family home in Gary, Indiana. The band played gigs in local bars and pubs and the money Joseph made from the band supplemented his income from the steel mill job.

Contrary to what the media would have us believe, Michael and his brothers were never forced into music and entertainment by their father. Because the Jackson's siblings were born in a family with music in their genes, it was natural that they followed in the family's heritage. Irrespective of the above, the media continued to harp that Joseph Jackson forced his children to sing and dance. But why would the media adopt this line of the story? Well, the answer is simple-to titiltate the public into buying their newspapers. Describing Joseph as an abusive father was a very good and sensational shocking story which suited tabloids' type of 'exclusive' news. 'Abuse' is also a powerful term which resonates with many people and when it is linked to a popular family like the Jacksons, then a big story line is created and this is good for the celebrity intoxicated public. It was the tabloids which made some people believe that Joseph Jackson abused and forced his boys to start singing and dancing. But this could not be further from the truth. While the media's version of the founding of Jackson 5 was a complete misinformation, their story line bordered on fabrication and sensationalism. The truth of the matter was that the Jacksons siblings possessed the traits from their parents Joseph and Katherine who themselves were part time musicians when they were young.The children simply inherited the music genes that flowed in the blood of their immediate parent's and that of their grand and great grand parents as well.To confirm the above, Jermaine Jackson wrote in his book 'Michael, Through a Brother's Eyes': *"When our parents met in 1949, their individual DNA must have combined to create some kind of super-gene for our musical inheritance. It was no accident of birth"*. Michael before he passed away also said that their parents' marriage was a divine union of two persons who were in music and dance.

Joseph Jackson simply harnessed the talent that were evident in his children as they started to mess around with his coveted guitar in the 1960s. Before he eventually discovered their prank after they broke his guitar, his children were already quite ahead in their quest to become musicians. After he found out that they broke his guitar, he was not angry but went out and bought a new one and began to coach his boys in their tiny house at Gary, Indiana. As regards Michael, he was naturally blessed with singing which from a very young age of five years old got his father's attention. Joseph Jackson inspite of all the things the the media might accuse and blame him for, foresaw the natural talent that was brewing in his boys. So instinctively the patriarch began to concentrate and nurture his children and later drafted Michael to join his elder siblings. It was Joseph Jackson who later selected Michael as the lead singer and front man of Jackson 5. Joseph Jackson might have a been a bit harsh on him in particular but the intention was to make sure that Michael become the face of the family band, and boy, how right it turned out to be as later on in life he, Michael matured to become one of the greatest musicians ever to grace the world.

Joseph Jackson was born in a poor family and imbibed some of the regimented lifestyle in which he was raised. He did not know any other way and henceforth applied same style of upbringing to his children. He meant well for them and wanted to support them and their chosen career against a backdrop of black neighbourhood that was ridden with drugs and violence in the 1960s. Michael later said that his father might have made some mistakes in the strong way he brought them up but at the same time he also acknowledged that their father believed he was doing the best for the family in those days.

So, contrary to what the tabloids widely reported about the abuse of the Jackson brothers by their father Joseph in the days when they were growing up, their father's intention was to raise his children in the best possible way he could. He also had the premonition that his youngest son Michael who was only 5 years old at the time if well coached and supported, would become a superstar which he eventually became.The result of Joseph's tenacity and guidance was for his children to become the best boy band in the 1960s and not only did they achieve this, but they went on to become famous worldwide. Music kept the Jackson family together in those days as well as keeping them away from drugs and gangs which were rampant in America inner cities in the 1950s and 1960s.

Jackson 5 was formed in Gary, Indiana in 1963. Jackie, Tito, Jermaine and Marlon were been coached by their father to perform in the youth talent shows in their local school. But tiny Michael, who was the youngest brother at the time, was also showing interest in what was going on in the family. Joseph instinctively noticed that his youngest son Michael was showing a wonderful singing and dancing talent as well and wasted no time in drafting him into what his elder siblings were doing.Whether it was the master stroke of a genius or just by chance but Jackson Snr saw something different in his little boy. He therefore decided to immediately put Michael who was 5 years old at the time into what he, Joseph was putting together as a family band. While little Michael started off by sharing singing duties with Jermaine, he moved quickly to become the lead singer of the family band. Joseph and Katherine jointly encouraged their boys to work and be serious on their musical career. It is safe to say that the Jackson boys had already chosen to begin singing together before their parents took notice of them. After they were discovered, both father and mother threw all their support to their children. Whilst mum took care of the family chores with her daughters Rebbie and LaToya, Joseph would spend most of his time after work to coach the boys in rehearsals which starts immediately after they return from school. The rehearsals took place at their tiny family home on 2300 Jackson Street, Gary, Indiana. Joseph maintained a strict regime which the boys followed. The strict attitude of Joseph in coaching his children was later to be turned around by the media to mean that he was an 'abusive' father.

As the boys were developing their musical career, their father saved money from his meagre salary from his steel mill job to buy them new musical instruments. Joseph Jackson never missed a session of his children's rehearsals and whilst coaching them in music and dancing he did instil discipline and drummed it into their head that if they worked hard in the music business, the sky would be their limit. Looking back now on the success of Jackson 5 and the emergence of Michael later as a world super star, their father Joseph, no doubt, has now been proved right. Joseph Jackson single-handedly nurtured his boys and gave them the confidence to believe in their abilities to sing, dance and entertain. Joseph Jackson as his son Michael, later imbibed, was a perfectionist. Michael later said that one of the characteristics he picked up from his father which he applied to his career when he became a solo artist was beign a perfectionist! Joseph might have been strict with his boys but his aim was to make sure they become the best in the business which we all know they did. No matter what the tabloids wrote in those days and may continue to write in order to sell papers, Joseph Jackson is thoroughly vindicated today, especially when one look at what his children and especially Michael achieved in his lifetime.

Black neighbourhood in America in the 1960s

Life in America in the 1960s, especially for many inner city black families was tough. White collar jobs were difficult to come by and racism was also rife as civil rights movements occupied the best part of black Americans' psych at the time. In those days black families knew that one of the best ways they could make a decent living was through music which till this day has remained one area where black people still excel in America. Singing and dancing are in the DNA of African-Americans which could be traced to slavery. In Africa where the slaves came from, music is associated with traditional religion and ritual whorship of the gods. Every African from childhood is expected to know how to dance gracefully while making offerings to the deity or the orisha. Dancing by descedants of slaves as a way of appeasing orisha and other gods can still be noticed in many parts of the Caribbean and South America including Brazil, Cuba and other countries in the southern hemisphere. During the time of slavery in the Americas, black slave families would often be seen in the farms singing away while doing their work as it was back in Africa where the slaves came from 300 years ago. In Africa till this day, music is connected to ancient rituals and festivals during which locals sing and dance to the gods and singing and dancing are still part of every day life in Africa especially in the villages.

In America in the 1960s, black men and women including a whole family in some cases got involved in music and entertainment, for some as a regular career and for others, as a part-time job in order to supplement a family's regular income. In the case of Joseph Jackson, he delved into music first of all because his parents and grand parents sang in the farms and in the church, so the music DNA was in him. In turn he passed it on to his children and did encourage them to take it serious after he discovered that they were interested in music too. In those days, black parents would enrol their young children in a local music competition and talent shows, hoping that their offsprings would go from there to make a career for themselves. After Jackson 5 in the 1960s, other famous musicians who competed in their local neighbourhood talent shows and moved on to become successful include the late Whitney Houston, Beyonce and Usher among others. Joseph Jackson, with his music background and experience, had the foresight to believe in his children. So, in the back yard of his tiny house in Gary, Indiana, he would organize them after the infamous discovery that his children had been messing about with his guitar and got them down to preparing sons Jackie, Tito, Jermaine, Marlon and Michael to take part in local talent shows that were organised up and down their neighbourhood in those days. The talent shows in America in the 1960s were like the present day *'X Factor'* shows of Simon Cowell in England and America. Joseph Jackson was a great believer in talent shows in those days and did every thing possible to make sure his boys took part in the shows. The Jackson's siblings were thoroughly coached by their serious-minded father. They put all their energy in it and it was no surprise that the brothers won most of the competitions that were held in their neighbourhood. After beign successful in school and local competetions, they moved on to also perform in local clubs, pubs and on TV in their home town of Indiana. As their popularity grew, their father Joseph came up with a befitting stage name for them: "Jackson 5" which changed the life of the Jackson family forever. With their name now making rounds in America, they began to receive invitations to play in bigger clubs outside their town including in big cities such as New York and Chicago, the latter been the entertainment capital of America at that time.

As time went on, they got noticed by one of America's oldest and iconic recording studios, Motown. In those days, if you are a good black musician or band and you are not signed to Motown, then you are really nobody. So Jackson 5 was invited to the Motown studios in California after Berry Gordy moved Motown which was originally based in Detroit, Michigan to California. In the meantime as Jackson 5 was then earning good money, Joseph relocated his family from Gary, Indiana to California which made it easy for the band to get more bookings for show and get them closer to the recording studio Motown. After a set of auditioning with Motown, Jackson 5 got signed on by the recording studio.With time, the band went on to produce 5 best-selling albums and subsequently made a lot of money from record sales and live performances all over the world. Their first album *I Want You Back* went to no 1 in many countries. The story of the 5 young black boys from Gary, Indiana who can sing and dance became a worldwide phenomenon. Jackson 5 gradually developed into a wonderful boy band which people of all races, irrespective of their age group connected with because of their kind of music and entertainment style. And what made them more interesting and special was that they are brothers who can really sing, dance and work the crowd! As the band grew Joseph naturally assumed the role of manager. With his boys then successful beyond his imagination, he with the help of their recording studio Motown, proceeded to organise tours for Jackson 5 all over America and also took the band to tours in Europe. Their first visit to Europe was England to perform at the Royal Variety Show in 1969. And since that visit to England, the British baby boomers of the 60s till this day have not forgotten Jackson 5 and especially, Michael Jackson. As in America, Europe and other continents in those days, many people all over the world got sucked into the Jackson 5 groove.

The success of Jackson 5 turned the family's fortune round while also making them vulnerable to temptations of drug use and other dangers as gang violence. In those days, American inner cities were riddled with drug and gang violence. Joseph sensed that with the rapid success of Jackson 5, his children might get caught up in the fast life and drugs that were prevalent in American inner cities at the time. With the above in mind he came up with some stricter rules for his children. He introduced private schooling for the boys at home and would have a private teacher join them during tours. Rehearsals at home also became more intense and occasionally Joseph would 'draw' the belt to put the unruly ones in check. Michael who later grew up to be quiet and shy was actually the most naughty and mischievous one and would receive the harshest of punishments from his father. Joseph Jackson might have used a bit of a heavy hand on his boys but all he tried to do was to make sure that his children remained focused in their education and most importantly in their chosen musical career.

In his time, Joseph Jackson was brought up in a strict way by his conservative black descendant family and applied same method in raising his children. He didn't know any difference to how he was brought up. He might have been a bit harsh in raising his children the way he did however, it is not fair to describe his actions then as beign cruel as the media people have implied it over the years. But as Michael pointed out during a speech at Oxford University in England some time before he died, he said that his father might have made some mistakes then but that his actions were intended for the good of him and his siblings.

Some people who aim for success do tend to push themselves or their subjects to the limit, sometimes using unpleasant tactics and methods to achieve their objective. When he was in charge, Sir Alex Ferguson, the most successful manager in the history of Manchester United would often fly into a rage and lash out at his players if things were not going well during a football match. Some people interested in football might remember once during a football match when his team was loosing a crucial game, Ferguson at half time talk in the dressing room was very angry at his players and in a rage kicked a football boot which mistakenly hit and smashed David Beckham's face who at the time was his star player. Would you describe Ferguson as an abusive or wicked manager? Of course not, all he was trying to do was to stress a point and get the best out of his players. To Ferguson, his objective was for Manchester United to win that game which infact they went on and won at the final whistle. But the press in England fashionably dubbed Ferguson's action on that fateful day as *'bringing out the hair dryer'* which was a more mild description of his action on that day. Then for the same type of action but in different circumstances, Joseph Jackson got labelled as an abusive father. Why did the press choose 'abuse' for the Jacksons? Because they know that it connected to Michael Jackson, a mega star, whose story of abuse would resonate with people and help sell newspapers! Michael Jackson had enormous pulling power in selling sensational stories.

British tabloids led by the rogue and defunct *News of the World* concentrated on publishing sensational articles about Michael Jackson, his father and the rest of the Jackson family in order to increase the circulation of their newspapers. The irony was that many of the stories were based on lies and fabrications, dressed up as the truth. The tabloids knew that 'abuse' as the new post baby-boom crime word is shocking and in order to sell papers, it is the perfect term to describe a father who has strong character like Joseph Jackson. The tabloids exploited and capitalised on the Jacksons' abuse story to push for increase in the sales of their papers. But give people what they want and they will buy it. It's clear these days that the truth matters little anymore. People want to be incited and excited and they also want to read about gossips and sensationalism; more so, if it is connected to a celebrity. It doesn't matter to people if they are lied to; infact some people these days just to want to be lied to. The finer details are irrelevant as long as it is about a celebrity as big as Michael Jackson.

The media often pretend to protect and inform us but in reality they are looking after their own interest. In some interviews which Michael gave to the media, he acknowledged the strict rules which his father put in place during the formative years of Jackson 5 but never used the word 'abuse' to describe his father. Michael, his brothers and youngest sister Janet bar LaToya, have said on many occasions that although their father was strict with them when they were growing up but that they do not consider him as an abusive or wicked father. All of them have reiterated that their father did what he did to make sure that they did not fall into the wrong hands in their neighbourhood in those days. They have also said so at different occasions, in interviews and books respectively. They have all acknowledged that their father's intention at the time was to make sure that they remained focused in their chosen music and entertainment career. All of the Jacksons bar LaToya have maintained that it was the press who manufactured the word 'abuse' to describe their father.

Michael once said that music was what he and his brothers did for entertainment. He confirmed that his father was very strict, working with them on their music, and critiquing their performance at home every day after school. He said he sang and danced and that it was so natural for him that it felt like drawing a breath of air and exhaling it. He also maintained that he got into music because it is what he wanted to do from when he was 5 years old and that he was not forced by anybody to do it. He said that the family's love for music kept them together in those days and that their father crucially nurtured them to become the best. As for Michael in particular, when he was with Jackson 5 and when he went solo and lived on his own, a reliable source close to him told me that *"in a minute if he wanted, he would come up with a sound bite and dance style to go with it. For Michael, music was an instinctive force in his life and it was what he wanted to do in life."* But irrespective of this, Michael's view of how and why he chose music as a career have been taken out of context and twisted around by the media to give the impression that he was forced into music by his father, Joseph. The media's version sounds tittilating for readers and that was the reason why they constantly published that Michael Jackson was 'abused' and 'forced' to sing and dance. The week Michael died, the tabloids got people more incited by reprinting once again of the abuse he suffered from his father.'*News of the World*' used the phrase several times to embellish their 16-page souvenir tribute to Michael when he died in 2009. However, according to one former Jackson staff member who spoke to me on condition of anonymity: "*I can tell that none of us who were close to Michael or any member of his family was impressed with that silly tribute from the British newspaper. Michael actually hated 'News of the World' because of all the horrible things they wrote about him when he was alive*". Now Michael didn't need to worry from his grave though because as as fate would have it, some years after his death *News of the World* was forced to close down after they were exposed as a fraud.

In the modern egalitarian world, 'abuse' has become a cool choice of word which does catch peoples' attention whenever it is included as part of a celebrity's story. A celebrity claiming to have been 'abused' when young or suddenly coming out to tell the world that he or she is gay have become good publicity stunt. It is the trend these days from America to Britain to see a wannabe celebrity who wants easy publicity to go to a tabloid and claim that he or she was abused sometime in the past. And if the abuse was supposedly carried out by the 'victim's' father, a famous musician, actor, former teacher, ex-boyfriend or famous footballer, then the story would attract more interest from the tabloids because it is the type of sensationalism which sale newspapers. The 'victim' might be rubbish at what he or she does as a career but in order to promote a new film, sell music, book or simply to seek for fresh publicity as the 'victim's' sale by date might have passed, the tabloid is the place they go to rejuvenate him or herself. The tabloids are not interested because they have any sympathy for the 'victim' but because the story would increase sale of their newspapers. So what we are seeing in this day and age of narcissism is cheap publicity from wannabe celebrities who are using 'abuse' and the media to promote their goal.

Susan Boyle, one time *Britain Got Talent* star does not by any means fall into the above category as she is hugely talented in her own right. But sometime ago she revealed that she was abused at school. Susan didn't reveal this tragic aspect of her life when she contested in the talent show and sold out her initial albums. The story of her abuse emerged some years after as she probably needed some publicity to promote and sell her new album which came out after a couple of years of inactivity. Susan might truly have been abused at school as she said but without her revelation many years afterwards, she would still have made success of her new album because she is no doubt a very talented singer. British soft porn model, Katie Price aka Jordan once claimed that she was raped by a former male friend. But after initially speaking to a tabloid about it, no further details emerged from her, even after being pressed by the media to tell more about her ordeal. Sheryl Gascgoine ex-wife of British football star Paul Gascgoine once also claimed that she was raped several times by her former husband, Paul. Sheryl broke the story when she was trying to promote her book which was essentially a memoir about her marriage to Paul. But after Gazza threatened to sue, all went quiet. After many years of keeping the tragic story of rape to themselves, some other ladies who include Joan Collins, Ulrika Johnson and Rita Ratzen have also revealed that they were raped sometime in the past.

But why is it that if a person was raped and felt traumatised as is expected, he or she goes to the tabloid after many years have passed, instead of going to the police? In America Bill Cosby is alleged to have raped some women who worked with him many years ago.

Again one cannot understand how mature and well enlightened women would decide to keep quiet for many years after a terrible thing like rape happened to them and then suddenly wants to talk about it. Could it be that some of them suddenly remembered their ordeal because they have some products to promote, sell or may be use rape to maximize their fledging popularity? In our modern voyeuristic society, rape and abuse stories have been published very often by the tabloids and mainstream newspapers, some without verification or cross-checking of facts as happened to Sir Richard Cliff, that the public are becoming desensitized about it.

Michael Jackson never intended to use his father's strictness to score any cheap publicity neither did he ever use the word 'abuse' to describe his father's action on him and his siblings when they were growing up. What Michael wrote in his book *Moonwalk* about his father's strictness was simply a narrative of how he and his siblings grew up in a disciplined environment. Joseph wanted his children to reach the height he aspired for them in music and entertainment and used some strict rules to ensure that they concentrated on rehearsals at home instead of running about on the streets like other children in their neighbourhood at the time. As is history now, Joseph Jackson achieved the aim he set for himself as a father and the height he wanted his children to reach. As we all saw afterwards, Jackson 5 and Michael Jackson his youngest son, by the 1960s were already household names. So therefore credit to Joseph Jackson who did not take his eyes off from him and his brothers while they were growing up. Michael did not need to remind the world that he existed, let alone use 'abuse' as a strategy to sell his book or music. It was the media that labelled Joseph Jackson as an abusive father. The objective of the media was simplyto create sensational headlines in order to sell newspapers and increase TV viewership.

CHAPTER THREE

JACKSON 5-*Emergence of an icon*

Jackson 5 was formed the day Tito broke their father's guitar

The press has often claimed that Joseph Jackson, the father of the Jacksons forced his boys into entertainment. This could not be further from the truth because the emergence of Jackson 5 was a combination of destiny and the adage which says that blood don't lie. In their youth and up to when they started a family, Joseph Jackson and his wife Katherine were also involved in music, albeit in an amateur way. That said, the two of them also had music flowing in their blood as both of their parents who were descdants of slave, also sang. When their children were young Joseph was a part-time musician earning extra cash which supplemented his regular income as a steel mill worker and his wife Katherine worked in a supermarket and in her spare time, sang in her local church. So music naturally ran in the Jacksons' family blood. From the eldest of Joseph's boys who is Jackie, to the youngest Michael, all can sing and or play one musical instrument or another. Michael in his own case always said that he inherited his soft voice and singing talent from his mother Katherine who was a chorister in her local church. So while Jackie, Tito and Jermaine played the guitar like their father Joseph, Michael leaned towards singing like their mother Katherine.

The story of Jackson 5 started when Jackie, Tito and Jermaine would often 'borrow' their father's coveted guitar from where he hid it in a closet and strummed away while singing songs they have heard on the radio. They played this prank for many months until their luck ran out one day. On that fateful day, Tito broke the strings of the guitar. Panic and fear gripped the boys because they thought that their father would surely '*give it*' to them when he returns home and find out what they have done to his guitar. But as fate would have it, what followed after their father found out was to change the Jacksons' family history and fortune forever. So when Joseph came back home one day and found out about his broken guitar, to the boy's amazement, after cautioning them lightly went out and bought a brand new guitar. On his return home, he beckoned the boys to come and show him what they can do with a guitar. He was surprised to see that Jackie, Tito and Jermaine can all actually play the guitar. To this day, the Jacksons children cannot quite comprehend why their father took a different approach to his usual attitude of lashing out. But according to a Jackson insider: "*It was destined that musical success would come out of a broken guitar and that Joseph's broken guitar would become the corner stone of the foundation of Jacksons 5. And who would ever have imagined that a broken guitar would turn the Jacksons to become one of the most famous families in the world? It is right therefore to give credit to Joseph Jackson for having the vision, foresight and excellent judgement to spot the talents that were brewing in his young children at the time.*"

From the day Joseph bought a new guitar and called his boys together, he effectively began to organise auditions and rehearsals for them at their tiny home in Gary, Indiana. All the elderly brothers took part. Michael was the youngest at the time and initially Joseph didn't think he was mature enough to join his older brothers in the rehearsals. But at less than 5 years old then, he refused to watch from the side. So whenever his older brothers were rehearsing, he would put together some cardboard cartons in one corner of the house and announce that those were his drums. He would sit there while rehearsals were going on and start banging away on his make-shift 'drums'. Joseph would rehearse all aspects of music with his sons, teaching them also how to perform and work the crowd. His experience as a part-time musician helped him guide his sons through the formative years of Jackson 5. In those days, as family rehearsal would be underway young Michael would sometimes also go to one corner of the room and begin to sing. Typical of Joseph, he quickily noticed that his youngest son could really sing. Wasting no time, he drafted Michael into the group and placed him as the front man and lead singer of the then amateur band. By the age of 5, Michael had become the voice and face of the group. Whenever they took part in their neighbourhood talent shows and or performed in local clubs, pubs and on TV, people where perplexed to see this tiny little black boy strutting around the stage and singing some adult songs, sometimes even better than the original artist who made the songs!

Recalling the formation of Jackson 5 in the early 1960's as described above, one would see a big contrast to what the tabloids have published in the past about Joseph forcing his children to sing and dance. Rather the Jackson boys have all said that they '*felt driven*" by their father and '*not pushed*" and that they were '*guided to where they wanted to go*" in their chosen career. As every responsible father who wishes the best for his children would do, Joseph Jackson instilled discipline in his boys so that they could remain focus in those days. He told them that it was going to be "*blood, sweat and tears-if they wanted to become the best in the busines.*" This discipline and hard work were the guiding principle which helped Michael to produce some great albums such as *Off the Wall, Thriller, Bad and Dangerous* in later years when he went solo. His natural talent aside, without the graft Joseph instilled in Michael, would he have become the superstar he was before his death? Who knows?

After winning several local talent show competetions in which their father entered them in those days in Gary, Indiana, Jackson 5 moved on to be performing in cities around United States and on TV. In the process they got spotted and signed on with Motown recording studio which propelled them to another level. The group quickly moved with their new recording label, Motown to release 2 initial albums in the 1960s. *'I Want You Back'*, which was released in 1965 and *'ABC'* in 1969 both of the albums which kept people dancing for many months, if not years. The two albums sold more than 5 million copies worldwide respectively. As Michael was the lead singer, the albums also made the world take notice of his singing talent and established him as a super star in the making from that very early age.

In those days, while touring with his brothers and opening shows for established stars such as Fred Astaire, Sammy Davies Jnr, Frank Sinatra, and James Brown in places such as Chicago which was the entertainment centre of America at the time, Michael would concentrate on watching the stars as mentioned above and study how they danced and worked the crowd. Some of the things the stars did on stage captured Michael's imagination and when he had some private moment and alone, would try to imitate what he had seen while adding his own element too. *'These showmen'* as he later described them, were all very inspirational to him. Their music, dance moves and the things they did on stage captivated him. Michael later said in his book *Moonwalk* after the breakup of Jackson 5 that he would carefully watch the stars in those days because he wanted to learn from them-the way they danced, held the microphone and worked the crowd. He said he was particularly fascinated by James Brown from whom he learnt how to move his feet, grunt and spin and turn on stage.The performances of James Brown, Sammy Davies Junior, Fred Astaire, Gene Kelly among others were all inspirational to young Michael then. And after he left Jackson 5 to go solo, watching his moves on stage, it was not difficult to see that Michael actually incorporated all the acts he picked up in those days in his dance move and stage performances later in his career. As he confessed after he became successful, he often imitated James Brown by skidding across the stage during performances.

Although Michael was the youngest of the brothers

when they were all in Jackson 5 but he became very influential in most of the decisions that needed to be made at the time in their music which ranged from the lyrics of their music to the choreography and stage costume they would wear during performances. Inspite of being the youngest, people around the band including their father Joseph and his brothers soon realised that Michael was naturally talented and knew the best way to carry the band forward, so they allowed him. After Jackson 5 broke up, Michael confirmed his 'leadership' of the band by saying that age should not be a barrier and that people should listen and acknowledge those around them who have the talent and know-how to make things happen. He was referring to himself. Michael was the 'leader' then and it didn't matter that he was the 'baby' of the group, his advice was critical to the success of Jackson 5.

He was also the main attraction in those days as many teenage fans and adults alike wanted to meet and take photographs with him whenever and wherever the Jacksons performed. At the height of the band'spopularity in America, thousands of young people would often gather in advance, sometimes waiting for long hours and days, to get into the auditorium where Jackson 5 was playing. Although people loved the group however, many of them in particular wanted to see their favourite Jackson who happens to be the young Michael. Wherever the Jacksons performed, the air in the hall would often be filled with chants of *Michael, Michael.* Some fans would be shedding tears, almost fainting in a bid to get his attention. People who followed Michael in his adult life may have noticed as well that when he went on tours of Europe and Asia in the 1980s, women often wept and fainted when he was performing. Michael often joked that whenever he opens his mouth, music comes out. Being a religious man, he was always grateful to God to have honored him with the natural ability to sing. Michael Jackson was born with immense natural musicality to share with the world and he felt very privileged by it.

The break up of Jackson 5

As was inevitable, the Jackson boys began to grow up, each having a regular girlfriend, getting married and later moving out of the family home at Encino, California. The brothers' wanted to start their own respective families and as this development was taking place, their commitment to Jackson 5 naturally began to wane. Although Michael knew that one day he would be moving on as a solo artist but the sudden separation from each other and setting up of different homes by his elder brothers made his decision more imminent. As the dynamic of the band was changing and each brother now to his own the bond that held them together naturally began to crack. Although the Jackson brothers were each other's 'friend' however, it was no secret in those days that Michael was closest to Jermaine. When Jermaine met and married Berry Gordy's daughter in 1979 and moved out of the Jacksons' family home, Michael was devastated. Berry Gordy was the founder and owner of Motown Recods which introduced Jackson 5 to America and the rest of the world. He was also very close friend to the Jackson family and had no problem marrying off his daughter to one of the Jacksons. With Jackie, Tito, Jermaine and lastly Marlon getting married and moving out of the family home Jackson 5 effectively disintegrated.

Emergence of an icon

Although Michael was very much affected by the turn of events with his family band, however, it turned out to be a blessing in disguise for him because he then found solace in his loneliness by writing and composing new songs. He also had the time then to begin to experiment with new dance steps incorporating also some of the things he had seen Fred Alstaire, Sammy Davies Jnr and James Brown do on stage when he was with Jackson 5 in the early days. Now that the family home was empty without the brothers,

Michael would dance for hours in front of the mirror and occasionally call on his youngest sister Janet who was still at home at the time to critique him.

Meanwhile, Berry Gordy owner of Motown who was also an experienced talent spotter and record producer in his own right in those days, had already identified Michael as the most talented of the Jackson brothers. For Berry Gordy, Michael was actually the real deal in Jackson 5. Even though one of the Jacksons, Jermaine had married his daughter, to Gordy, the slow break up of Jackson 5 was a blessing for his business too because he moved quickly to support Michael in his endeavour to go solo and actually encouraged him to do so immediately. Gordy threw his weight behind Michael and together after a short period of the break up of Jackson 5, teamed up to work, produce and release Michael's first solo album entitled *Got ToBe There* in the fall of 1979. Although not a massive hit by Michael's standard the album still did quite well and paved the way for his solo stardom. From the 1980s to the middle of the century, the Jackson brothers were still together and performing from time to time but after the brothers respective marriages, the centre could not hold together anymore and by the mid 1980s, the curtain was drawn and Jackson 5 was effectively finished as a band. From then onwards Michael never looked back in his solo career and went on to produce some world class albums which landed him the title of King of Pop as we all came to know him before his death in 2009. During his solo career, he also collaborated with the likes of Quincy Jones, a respected song writer and music producer with whom they achieved great things together. It is said that Michael's collaboration with Quincy Jones changed the face of pop music forever.

After leaving Jackson 5 and producing his first album-*Got To Be There* with Berry Gordy, he moved on to work with Quincy Jones. The next time Michael Jackson emerged it was to be with an album that got the world dancing. *Off the Wall*, with other songs-*Don't Stop Till*

You Get Enough including *Billy Jean* were a master class in composition and production. Subsequent album that followed, *Thriller* was to be an album that till this day has remained one of the best selling albums in history. *Thriller* reached a sales record that no other album by any musician living or dead, ever reached. From an early age Michael had a goal to develop a global hit with the highest ever possible record sales. He said that *Thriller* was a landmark in his life and that he was proud of it. Reaching the goal he aimed for himself with the album meant that a child star could grow to revolutionise music and achieve worldwide status and creating a popular music trend and dance moves which till this day is followed by millions of young people all over the world. With *Thriller*, Michael achieved his life dream. *Thriller* made him very wealthy but it was also one of the sources of some of the troubles he later had in life.

As the talent continued to burn in Michael, other albums such as '*Bad*' and '*History*' quickly followed all of which combined with *Thriller* made his friend Elizabeth Taylor to be the first person to give him the title of *King of Pop*. In his solo career, Michael's music earned him success, incredible wealth, fame and influence so much so that by the late1980s, Michael Jackson was better known around the world than Coca-Cola and computer. Success and wealth might have been the perfect reward for Michael's talent and hard work but they also brought about his downfall. The problems that dogged his life because of his success and wealth were some of the main reasons for writing this book. As his life was turned upside down and opened up to public scrutiny, Michael lamented that becoming public property was very hard to take even though it was due to the success of his music.

In the research of this book, I came to realize that Michael Jackson as a private individual was very different to Michael Jackson the musician and entertainer. Although music, performing and entertainment were his life but Michael was a guy who in private spoke very softly and was extremely shy too. He was a child star and was naturally talented but unfortunately his talent and the success he derived from it became a curse in disguise. While some of us adored him he became the envy of others who plotted his down fall. Then gold diggers moved in as well to exploit him from the wealth he made through his music. After he became successful and extremely wealthy, control of his life and to an extent, his career went out of his hands. The public and the media celebrated Michael Jackson but also contributed immensely to his misery and early demise. His identity as a successful musician and entertainer also tied him to be a money making machine for others.

After the break up of Jackson 5 and going solo with 3 successful albums, his fame and success became a worldwide phenomena and in order to reach out to some part of the world Jackson 5 did not quite reach in those days, Michael decided that his father would not be able to cope with the direction his career was moving so he terminated his father's managerial role with him and moved on to appoint professional public relations people including lawyers who would look after his music and entertainment business including promoting his worldwide tours. Joe Jackson had been managing his childrens' career since the 1960s but as his son was now breaking records with his new brand of music, it was inevitable that father and son must go their separate ways. Michael's former staff told me: *'although he was already well known around the world but as a perfectionist, he was still not satisfied. His aim was to become the best that there could ever be, to conquer the world and to reach places around the world where Jackson 5 with all their popularity in those days never penetrated.''* So after more than two decades with his father as manager, Michael decided to terminate his working relationship with Joseph Jackson. To Michael at that time, his father was not the man to take him to the height he was aiming for in his career. To be able to conquer the world musically, some fresh ideas and a new direction were needed. As he didn't want to upset his father by dumping him, Michael later released a statement. *"Relieving my father as my manager didn't mean anything bad in my heart, I don't know if it did in his heart, but it certainly didn't in mine."* Both father and son came to the conclusion that going solo and reaching out to the most remote part of the world required a different kind of approach. So as I was reliably informed, Joseph took it in his stride and moved on. The severance of tie between father and son went rather smoothly. Therefore all the negative things that were written by the tabloids about the tension that existed between Michael and his father were mostly lies and fabrications. People must remember that one of the ways in which tabloids generates sale of their papers is by printing lies and presenting them as truth. It is in their interest to create elements of shock that entices people to buy their newspapers. *The National Enquirer* USA and the British rogue and defunct *News of the World,* with the successor *Sun on Sunday* including their daily sister paper *The Sun* are masters of sensational journalism. In Britain you also have the *Daily Star* and the *Mirror* which are not much different to the ones above. Each one of these tabloids took turn in writing stories about Michael Jackson and his family that were unsubstantiated and in most cases based on fabrication.

Thriller transformed Michael's life long dreams into reality and made him very, very wealthy. More successes came with other albums *Bad* and *Dangerous* but as is the case with success and extreme wealth, they tend to turn peoples' head. As Michael became very successful, famous and influential, he also began to experiment with certain things that made some people and the media turn against him. His eccentricity which included engaging in numerous plastic surgeries, covering part of his face with handkerchief when he stepped out, being elusive and befriending young boys began to be the hallmark of the singer and all the above baffled the world.

According to Donald Trump, the side effects of the multiple plastic surgeries which Michael underwent after

Thriller began to make him loose confidence in meeting people as some things went wrong with his new physical appearance. In a CNN interview when Trump was running for President of America, he said that he loved Michael Jackson and had invited him and Lisa Marie Presley to his penthouse in Manhattan, New York to spend the weekend. Trump said that although Michael and Lisa Marie were staying just one floor above him but that he never saw them again until after several days later as Michael was quite shy of seeing any one. Trump noted that after the successes Michael achieved with his music he then went too far in transforming himself which led to a huge loss of confidence when it all began to go wrong.

Prior to *Thriller* however, Michael had already started to experiment with plastic surgery and 'making changes' to his skin, part of which began to develop white patches in some areas. As an adolescent at the time, he also had acute pimples on his face which bothered him very much. Acne is common with most teenagers but it was something that gave Michael Jackson sleepless nights especially as he saw himself as an entertainer and showman whose appearance must be impeccable. At the age of 19, Michael was already a well-known musician and entertainer and his duties included interacting regularly with fans and the general public. But he did not feel comfortable meeting people with pimples on his face. He also actually began to think of himself as an 'ugly' man. He didn't like his nose which he thought was big and flat. To him as a superstar, he had to look sexy and appealing especially to his younger fans was something he craved. Although Michael never denied his black heritage he did believe however, that he would be more appealing to his fans if got a softer-looking image by reshaping his nose and whitening his skin. To achieve his aim, he went under the knife several times after he had initially gone to raise his cheek bones just before *Thriller*. By the time the album *Bad* was released in 1997, Michael Jackson had completely transformed himself into a black-white 'zombie'. A source close to him at the time told me that soon after all the heavy plastic surgeries he went through, the side-effects began to manifest itself in his physical appearance, especially his nose which became fragile and that other parts of his body were also affected which impacted his general health. As questions were being asked about his transformation from black to 'white' he defended himself by saying that he had a big struggle to look at himself in the mirror in those days as his appearance was changing. He said he became very self-conscious about his appearance, particularly the changing colour of his skin and the pimples on his face. He also said that the white patches on his body impacted his mental state and that all of these messed up his personality. He confirmed that he was really embarassed to meet people with that state of condition of his skin. So he had no choice but to seek some remedies to alleviate the state of his skin condition.

Remarkably however, despite all the plastic surgery Micahel put himself through including 'messing' with his skin colour, sales of his albums and his popularity soared more and more. Nobody can deny that Michael Jackson was a very talented musician; you cannot take this away from him but one school of thought thinks that having plastic surgery to reshape his nose and lighten his skin colour probably made his younger and white female fans 'accept' him more. His brand of music, which is a mixture of pop, rock and ballads were also the type of music that is popular in white households. "*For white kids, Michael's new appearance just before 'Bad' was released resonated more with them*" a former staff told me.

After the series of plastic surgeries and glowing in his new appearance, Michael engaged in his 1987 world tour and the assumption was that he conquered the world then with his different kind of pop music and with a new physical appearance. After the tour he was crowned King of Pop, a title which no one dead or living would ever take away from him. Although he had transformed himself to a 'bimbo' with plastic surgery, nevertheless, he was still a black man who was better known than the president of his country at that time. To congratulate him on his successful world tour, he was invited to the White House for a private dinner and reception by President Ronald Reagan and his wife Nancy. He was guided on a tour of the the president's residence, had tea with the President and played the White House piano to the delight of the President and his wife. It is necessary to recall here that while a white American president gave Michael Jackson the recognition and respect he deserved for promoting America, the first black President of the country, Barack Obama failed to acknowledge and pay respect to the late King of Pop when he died in 2009. At least, to my knowledge, not before 24 hours passed did President Obama make any statement about Michael Jackson's passing.

Elvis Presley, The Beatles, Jimmy Hendrix, James Brown, Frank Sinatra, Bob Marley and Tupac, all might have been great in their own way as musicians but Michael Jackson was bigger than all of them. While time stood still upon his death on June 25 2009, *Thriller* became the first music video to be added to the National Film Archive of America after his death.

On the whole, what Michael achieved in his lifetime made him an icon, a legend and a 'brand' in itself which will be difficult to match by any other musician. Michael Jackson was a successful musician and became wealthy and famous through his chosen career. Some people also said that he became a prisoner of his success and one couldn't disagree with the assertion.

CHAPTER FOUR

KING OF POP

The success of Michael Jackson's albums, particularly *Thriller* made him a very wealthy and influential man. He was the king of the music industry in those days. Michael Jackson was named the 'King of Pop' by his friend Elizabeth Taylor, a title which he will thus be known forever. A Michael insider told me: *"Michael was so powerful and influential in those days that he could easily get an audience with any wealthy individual or powerful politician in any country from all over the world. All he had to do was ask"*.

From the mid 1980s leading up to mid 1990s, Michael was earning about one million dollars a day from his music and related merchandise world wide. To date it is said that he was the only musician in the world who has earned more than one billion dollars from music alone. The wealth he was generating from music and live shows put him in a different league from other musicians during his time. In those days, Michael was the guest of many rich people and celebrities in and outside America. At the height of his opulence and influence, Michael was dining with presidents, kings, queens and Arab sheiks. In America, beside President Ronald Reagan who hosted and had tea with him at the White House after his return from a very successful world tour in 1987, his other friends in those days too included President Bill Clinton and his wife Hilary who also hosted him at the White House. And outside of politics his other friends include Hugh Hefner the founder of *'Playboy'* magazine, Stephen Alan Wynn the king of the Casino industry, the late actor Marlon Brando, late actresses Elizabeth Taylor and Katherine Hepburn, late showmen Sammy Davies Jr, Fred Astaire and Liza Minelli among many others who ruled Hollywood and Chicago nightlife in those days. Everybody who mattered in Hollywood in those days wanted to be his friend or at least, be seen with him. Describing Michael Jackson as a 'celebrity' is an understatement. Michael Jackson is the real deal, one hell of a celebrity! It makes me think that the world has gone mad when talentless people such as Paris Hilton and the Kardashians are described as celebrities.

With his special brand of pop music, Michael Jackson appealed to people of all cultures. His music also broke down racial barriers. He was the first black artist who single-handedly paved the way for black musicians to be featured on MTV. *New York Times* hailed him as *"A one-man rescue team for the music business, a songwriter who has paved the way and set the direction for black artists for the present decade and for future generations, a dancer with the fanciest feet and singer who cuts across all boundaries of taste, style and colour ".* Michael's legacy will be felt for generations to come. And in order to preserve his memory, his music and videos have been documented and preserved at the American Library of Congress and the National Archives. Michael Jackson launched many trends in the music and fashion industry which went viral and are still followed by the public to this day.They include people wearing gloves as a fashion statement and some musicians wearing gloves too and clutching their crotch when performing on stage-just like the King of Pop did in those days. Although Michael admitted that he was not the originator of the *Moonwalk* dance but perfected the street dance which later became his signature dance move. *"Yes, You Can,* a slogan which Barack Obama changed to *"Yes We Can"* during his 2008 presidential campaign was a phrase that was coined by Michael Jackson. Another one of his phrases that has gone viral today is *"This Is It",* which was to be used as a theme for his ill-fated concert that was planned for August 2009 in London which unfortunately he did not live to perform.

Michael Jackson was a little boy who was blessed with natural talent and simply wanted to sing, dance and entertain. From when he was young, Michael was a very shy person but it was difficult to notice this aspect of him because whenever he went on stage to perform and work the crowd, he showed up with a completely different personality. As he described some musicians and dancers in the 1960s, he himself was also *'showman'* but after the show, he was always looking forward to having very private time of his own. According to my source *"If Michael could give his best during a concert (and he always did) to the the fans who had gone to see him and afterwards disappear to another planet until his next show, he would do so"*. Michael was always a shy person and when he was younger and in Jackson 5, was shielded by his father and brothers and this meant that his extreme shyness could not be particularly noticed but as he grew older, moved out and was making lot of money, the media intensified their pursuit of him. He could not handle the aggressiveness of the media and this made him very frustrated. Although he had the security around him and it was not easy for the paparazzis and others to get near to him but Michael still felt loss of his privacy by the media's intrusion. It might sound contradictory, especially for a person who said that he wanted to achieve goals and reach a landmark in music and entertainment but what he did not take into account was that his life and career would surely attract the media and people's interest about his daily life.

Michael just loved to entertain; money and popularity were not the main reasons why he went into music. But the question however remains, can someone achieve the the type of goals Michael achieved and not become a person of interest to the public? Success and fame unfortunately comes with burden and price.The goals Michael set for himself and which he very successfully reached, made people across the globe recognise him and his music and made them also take interest in whatever he was doing.

When Michael went solo in mid 1980s the world had already become a different society, a society that is mad with celebrity culture and supported by aggressive media. Mainstream electronic and print media found themselve competing with the tabloid section of the press and each one of them looking for ways to capture and retain readers and viewers. Some tabloids went a step further as they began to engage in criminal activities which included the tapping of telephone system of private indviduals and celebrities while also entrapping and stalking others in order to obtain 'exclusive' information and images which they will use to embellish the articles they intend to publish.To accomplish their objective and beat each other, most of the media organizations began to use paparazzis who are encouraged to pursue celebrities (sometime to their death as happened to Princess Diana) in order to obtain photos and news. Paparazzi pay masters include the *National Enquirer* in America and *News of the World* (defunct), *Sun on Sunday* and its daily sister paper *The Sun; Daily Star* and the *Mirror* in Britain. With these tabloids, the world of sensationalism as we know it today is now here to stay. Rupert Murdoch's tabloids and others were always ready and may still be in the act to pay huge sums of money to buy what they call 'exclusive' stories and images and this has fueled the illegal activities of paparazzis. Starting with ordinary people who have stories to sale, celebrities, footballers and politicians whose stories would generate wide circulation and readership are all targets of the of tabloids and the paparazzis.

Michael Jackson was a big game because his name and photos were headline-grabbing news and generated plenty of money for the tabloids. *News of the World, Sun on Sunday* and its daily sister paper *The Sun* found Michael Jackson's name difficult to resist and made a lot of money from selling stories about him. From the 1980s up to the day he died, Michael Jackson was at the top of the list of celebrities whose stories and or photos would escalate a bidding war between tabloids and media agencies who were willing to pay huge amount of money to paparazzis and private individuals that had any stories and images of him which they would then splash as 'Exclusive News' in the front pages of their paper. Although Michael had been a child star from the 1960s and had been interacting with the public and the media since he was 5 years old but when he moved out to live on his own, the 'protection' which his family provided him when he was with Jackson 5 was gone. On his own after Jackson 5 broke up, he was exposed to the machinations of the 21st century paparazzi and their media masters that paid them to harrass people like him. He moaned very much of how his life was turned into a public property. He complained to some of his closest staff members that his privacy had been badly invaded and was very upset about it.

The relentless media intrusion in his life started in earnest when he underwent his first plastic surgery in the early 1980s. As he began to mature as an adult and became famous, Michael became worried and concerned about his physical appearance. The acute acne he developed as an adolescent affected his confidence. Although he continued to appear in public to perform but privately whenever he returned to his room and looked in the mirror, he didn't like what he saw which were the spots on his face and the black and white patches (vitiligo disease) which started to appear on other parts of his body. As he was making plenty of money and mingling with celebrities in Hollywood at that time, he convinced himself that he had to do something about his appearance. People loved Michael Jackson the way he was but he thought he would make himself more appealing to his friends in Hollywood, majority of who were white by under going plastic surgery and whitening his natural black skin. He wanted to appear impeccable. Celebrities such as Elizabeth Taylor, Joan Collins and many others had done plastic surgery and Michael thought they all looked great. So he decided to join the bandwagon. He went for operation to lift his cheek bone, reshape his nose and as I was told, also whitened his skin which he later he denied. By the time he came out with the *Bad* album, Michael had completely transformed himself into some sort of half-black-half-white man. He may have deluded himself with thinking that after the surgeries he looked great but his appearance which was remarkably different to the black man he was before he came out with *Bad* prompted press speculation. There was also the story which was circulating at the time that he bought an oxygen chamber to sleep inside so that he won't get old! The latter story was a big fallacy as there was no oxygen chamber at his home in those days but as I have been reliably informed, Michael at the time had some health problems because of the plastic surgeries he did. *"After Michael's plastic surgeries there was the disfiguring of his facial structure. He also had problems with his cheek bones and nose which unfortunately began to give way".* A mole told me. When Michael died in 2009, looking at his corpse he was really unrecongnisable when compared to the cute black boy who sang *ABC* in the1960s. After all those plastic surgeries, Michael knew himself that he was not in the best of shape and to hide the damage from the plastic surgeries, he straightened his hair to cover part of his face and also used handkerchief to cover his nose whenever he went out in public.

As Donald Trump his friend pointed out, Michael's confidence was affected after all the plastic surgeries he went through. When he went to spend a weekend at Trump's place in New York, he was only seen on arrival and no one saw him and Liza Marie again until after several days. Speaking on TV several years after his death, Trump said that he hosted Michael at his block of apartments in New York in the same building where he, Trump lives but never saw Michael again until after several days. Apparently Michael preferred to spend time on his own to avoid coming in close contact with people because of the complications that was noticeable on his face and body. About that time too, he would also avoid seeing some of his personal staff unless he had put on makeup to cover the discrepancies on his face and skin, a reliable source told me. *"Most times after any meal, Michael would immediately retreat to his private quarters and would not be seen again until the following day.*

Although am not suggesting that he had any sexual intention towards children but in those days he prefered to spend time with young teenagers and his own children, Prince, Paris and Blanket because he felt that they were the people who would not judge his appearance". My source told me.

About his famous home *Neverland,* I was told that the original idea of building it was borne out of his insecurity with the outside world. Michael lost his childhood from a very tender age as he was heavily involved with Jackson 5. He was drafted into the family band when he was less than than 5 years old and he experienced some positive and negative things which most children of his age would never experience at that age. As he grew up and became wealthy, he wanted to reclaim the childhood he felt he lost while travelling all over the world with Jackson 5. So with his new found wealth he started toying with the idea of creating a home which would also serve as a playground for him, his children and his teenage friends. Although an adult by the time he was making lot of money, fairy tales, children stories and Disneyland still fascinated Michael Jackson.

When he lived at Encino, California it was almost impossible to step out of *Haveynhurst,* his family home because of the paparazzis and overzealous fans who would constantly camp daily outside the house to have a glimpse of him or the other members of the Jackson family. So as he made the money later on to build a home which would be designed as a fortress, he came up with the idea of building not just a fortified home but a fairy tale one too. He also wanted it to be located some where far away from the urban population. So he acquired a ranch in the Santa Ynez valleys of California where he built *Neverland* as his home then was known. *Neverland* was well secured with high walls and many other security systems so that he could have his privacy and let in only people that would have been thoroughly vetted. *Neverland* was one of Michael's life dreams. It was a dream he accomplished but a dream that also partly brought him down. His last accusation of sexually molesting a minor in 2003 which brought him and his brand crashing down was alleged to have been committed at *Neverland*. After the case was dismissed without finding him guilty, Michael never moved back to go and live there.

CHAPTER FIVE

THE PRICE OF STARDOM

Fame can either make one happy or miserable depending however, how a person handles it. Considering the number of stars and celebrities who have succumbed to the pressures of fame, it is easy to agree that fame can be counter productive. Marilyn Monroe, Jimi Hendrix, Kurt Corbaine, Whitney Houston and later Prince, all of them succumbed to the pressure of fame just like Michael Jackson.

Michael liked being a private person but also enjoyed the influential status his talent brought him. As a mega star, he had a conflict of how to deal with the media and the individuals who wanted a part of him as well as remaining private. The media in particular made him mad. You would realise that the world has gone mad when a group of men and women better known as paparazzis would decide to camp outside someone's property for days and nights in an effort to obtain unauthorized photographs and or images which they would they would then sell to the highest bidder in the media. Michael Jackson faced the paparazzis on a daily basis. They made his life a hell. But not only Michael Jackson mind you, the imbeciles have in their quest to obtain unauthorized images, also upset many celebrities. It was the paparazzis who chased Princess Diana and her boyfriend Dody Al Fayed to their death in an underground bridge in Paris in 1997. For Michael Jackson, they harassed him into depression. While some of the paparazzis have been taught a lesson by stars like Mike Tyson as he once knocked one of them out, others have continued to harass celebrities in order to make money out of their illicit activity.

1980s to the 1990s was the period Michael Jackson was on top of his game. He was the most popular person on earth at that time. Although he underwent plastic surgeries and looked anything but a black man nevertheless, no black man, living or dead was greater than him during that time. In 1997, Guiness World Book of Records declared him as the most famous person in the world. With his achievement and wealth it was obvious that his private life would fuel tabloid speculations. And because he was a person of interest to the world, any story about him was bound to titillate the public. Hence the paparazzis and the rest of the media organizations pursued him every where he went and poked their nose in every thing he did. Michael Jackson was no doubt a very big source of making money for the media, so from America to England, they exploited his name and image and continued to do so even after his death in order to keep selling newspapers and pulling viewers. To the media and especially the tabloids, any story about Michael Jackson was *exclusive* news.

The media, with complete acquiescence of the voyeuristic public, do create celebrities (although Michael Jacskon earned his own celebrity status) but also brings them down. Meanwhile, the tabloids don't like it when a celebrity ignores them because they always want to write some thing about a big celebrity every day or week so that they could continue newspapers. Princess Diana and Michael Jackson in those days were the 'darlings' of the tabloids because their life stories provided the tabloids with the opportunity to fabricate stories and make big sales every week. But as Diana and Michael decided to do certain things in private without involving the tabloids, they became 'enemies' of the tabloids respectively.

Money and success did not bring happiness to Michael Jackson instead it caused him heartbreak. From some of his private scribbles which were shown to me, he continuosly complained of unhappiness and loss of privacy because of the paparazzis. After Michael went solo and came out with world class albums which included *Off the Wall*, *Thriller, Bad and History* all of which made him incredibly wealthy, gold diggers encouraged by the media and the establishment in America turned his life into a circus that was played out in public. Media inquisition and other personal troubles which included several legal cases against him made Michael a very miserable man. He said that after his string of successes he had very few friends and felt very isolated and lonely. He recalled how occasionally he would run out in his neighbourhood in those days under some disguise to look for someone to talk to, just anybody who would want to be his friend, not because he is Michael Jackson but because he is a human beign! He wished for the basic stuff in life which had eluded him because of his success.When performing live shows Michael was a different person and would do whatever was necessary for the people who had paid to come and see him enjoy themselve. But afterwards he couldn't wait to retire to a quiet life and have a private time with personal friends (although he didn't have many in those days) and not be bothered by paparazzis and or the media. Some people have many facets of themself and Michael Jackson was no different. When he performed he was in total control of the stage and loved every minute of it but he also craved for some peace before the next show. He actually liked to meet genuine people to talk to but unfortunately he didn't have the type of true friends he wanted.

Music brought Jackson unrivalled wealth beyond what any other musician during his time ever achieved. At the height of his success between 1987 and 2003, he was worth more than $1 billion in assets and cash. For all the pomp and pageantry associated with musicians, few if any could be said to match the income he generated at the peak of his career. *Thriller* alone sold more than 100 million copies and remain until this day the biggest selling music album of all time. Michael Jackson's music appealed to all races and cultures. He cut across cultures by mixing blues and soul thereby creating his own version of pop music. He was awarded10 different world records in music by the Guiness World Book of Records. However, with all his achievements Michael Jackson became a marked man.

Some indviduals, including a section of the white media and the establishment in America became jealous of him. His profile as the greatest entertainer in the world was not accepted in some quarters. The strategy to bring him down was thus hatched.

*Making **Off The Wall** was one of the most difficult periods of my life, despite the eventual success it enjoyed. I had very few close friends at the time and felt isolated*
—**Michael Jackson**

CHAPTER SIX

MICHAEL JACKSON vs THE MEDIA –
How tabloids survive on blackmail and extortion

The media have always been used to spreading biased opinions, half truths, lies and fabrications in order to incite and entice the public. If you want to see sensationalism, gossip, slander and character assassination just look at the stories that were regularly published about Michael Jackson when he was alive and upon his death. The journalists who wrote the articles and their papers which published them would claim that they were disseminating news that needed to be reported. But distorting and fabricating information in order to increase newspaper sales is not right and it is not professional.

When Michael Jackson began to make lot of money and became a mega star, his relationship with the white media took a negative turn. Unfortunately he also became a victim of the competition that is still raging between traditional newspapers and tabloids which started since the introduction of computers and social networking sites in the past three decades or so. Internet and social media have negatively affected the circulation and sale of traditional newspapers and magazines. There has been a slow and steady decline in the sale of traditional newspapers and it is not getting better as more vibrant and different social networking sites are introduced. Owners of traditional newspapers have had to look for other ways of bringing back readers that have been deserting them and flocking to the internet and social media sites. The solution of the owners of traditional newspapers however, has been to introduce aggressive and sensational journalism. To support this strategy, the print press especially the tabloids have decided to throw all morals to the dogs. They now publish articles most of which could best be described as fabrications and half truths in order to titillate readers. It doesn't matter how they obtain their story, the sole aim of the tabloid press is to stay afloat and ahead of each other in the circulation and readership war that is going on between them. The competition between tabloids therefore and their aggressive way of gathering information have since taken print journalism to a whole new level. Led by the rogue and defunct *News of the World*, it's successor *Sun on Sunday* and their sister daily paper *The Sun* including others such as the *Mirror*, *The People*, *Daily Star* and *Sunday Sport* and across the Atlantic by their American counterpart *National Enquirer*, the public has continuously been fed with myriad of sensationalism about the life of celebrities with many of the stories dressed up as *exclusive news*. The tabloids say they are *'protecting society'* and that they are our *'moral guardian'* but what they are actually doing is protecting their own backside and making money by publishing sensationalism which they know would be of interest to the public and make people buy their newspapers.

In order to outwit each other as well and come out with exclusives, some tabloids have resorted to criminal activities such as spicing celebrities' drinks in order to entrap and force them to make confessions under the influence of alcohol. Some tabloids would also tap the telephone system of celebrities and dead teenagers! From 2011 to 2013, allegations of phone hacking engulfed many British tabloids, chief of them *News of the World*. The scandal that brought down the latter and nearly did so too with other papers began with the revelation in July 2011 that nearly a decade earlier, a private investigator hired by the *News of the World* had hacked into the mobile telephone and intercepted the voicemail of missing British teenager Milly Dowler who was later found dead in the woods. In spite of the newspaper knowing that the teenager was dead, they continued to publish messages stolen from her mobile phone and branded it *exclusive news*! When the crime was revealed in England, it shocked the nation. Amid a public backlash and withdrawal of advertising revenues from many companies and organizations in Britain and beyond, News International the parent company of *News of the World* on 7th July 2011, shut down the newspaper. British newspapers are not decent; they are cowards, hypocrites and bullies.

Advent of celebrity culture and the public's hunger for gossip about celebrities has given tabloids the opportunity to dupe society. They invade the privacy of individuals and defend it with the excuse that they are disseminating information. Unfortunately not only the tabloids engage in this nefarious activity, some online gossip websites, such as Twitter and TMZ in America have also emerged as celebrity gossip media organizations. They, like their newspaper counterparts, have also adopted the same strategy of gathering and disseminating sensationalism which most times they acquire through paparazzis and individuals whom they encourage to chase and harass celebrities.

When Michael Jackson was alive, hundreds of paparazzis depended on obtaining photos of him which they would sell to the media to make a living. At that time whenever his children who were appearing in public with their faces covered in veil stepped out with him, the hysteria among paparazzis would increase and sometimes put the Jacksons live in danger. According to one of Michael's former aide, *"paparazzis would often chase the family in motorcades in order to obtain photos of them and information of where they were going."* When Michael died in 2009, his children were made to emerge from behind the veil by the Jackson family. On one hand, the paparazzis were happy because it was the first time anybody outside of Michael's close circle got a view of what Prince, Paris and Blanket look like. But one of the paparazzis who often camped outside of Jackson's home in California told me this in confidence: *"I for one was disappointed that the Jackson family revealed the faces of the children at one go because I lost the opportunity to be the first to scoop some 'exclusive' photos of Michael*

Jackson's childrens' faces which could have fetched me lot of money". After the childrens' faces were revealed, the attention of the paparazzis turned fully then to the death of the childrens' father.

Michael Jackson was a victim of the 21st century tabloid press inquisition. When he was alive, he poured out his frustration to some of his very closest personnel. He was deeply troubled and pained by the intrusion of the media into his private life and wondered why newspapers and magazines would make up stories about him. Granted he was a mega star and that there was public appetite for stories about him, what he did not understand was the lies and fabrications that became part of every story that was printed about him. On several occasions, Michael would cry privately after reading some of the lies the newspapers had published about him. He did consider taking legal action in some cases but he also knew that if he sued, he would be giving the newspapers more publicity. Whilst talking to people close to him, I was reliably informed that he spoke sometimes to his mother Katherine to seek her advice and Katherine would often remind him that as long as he was a public figure, some garbage would continue to be written about him and that there was no need to take legal action against the newspapers. Though he heeded to his mother's advice but one thing that worried Michael was that once something negative is written and published about someone, whether true or false, the mud would stick and this is exactly what happened to him. As was evident after his death, the lies and fabrications written about him divided public opinion so much so that many prominent people who were his friends when the going was good deserted him on his death.

In spite of the distance he kept with the media, Michael tolerated some journalists and media personnel such as Oprah Winfrey whom he granted an interview in 1993 after 14 years of not giving any journalist the opportunity to interview him. But after he was hurt by Martin Bashir, who used him to make money and further his career, the singer completely shut the door once again for journalists and never gave any interview to any media organization until he died in 2009. The unfortunate thing however, was that Michael's ban on the media somehow extended also to his own family and the few friends he had at the time. As he wanted to reduce the gossip that was building around him, he cut off contact with everyone including members of his family and would often spend time on his own and in the company of his children. As I was informed by one of his former staff members: *"Michael would retire privately to his chambers, spend all day on his own without any food except for some orange juice, whilst trying to figure out what exactly he had done wrong to the world. His loneliness led him to become paranoid and very frustrated"* His body guards sometimes feared for the worst as they contemplated he might harm himself and would often tip toe to the door of his private quarters to listen in for any sign of life. Michael I am told experienced the worst period of his life from 2003 to 2009. With all the troubles around him, he felt that the world had abandoned him. Although it was no secret that he used some pain killing drugs in the past when he was burnt during the Pepsi Cola advert filming in Jan 1984, a habit he actually never got rid of, however, the situation he found himself between 2003 to 2009 made him increase the use of Propofol and Demerol to calm his nerves. As is with anti depressant drugs, he got hooked and made the situation worse by mixing them with the help of his doctor to very high propotions which then killed him. Meanwhile, before his death and as he was ebbing away slowly, the media applied more pressure by continuosly publishing some of the most outrageous garbages about him.

The tabloids were disappointed that Michael Jackson never went to jail for the child abuse allegations he was accused of over the years. Had he gone to jail, they would have had field day writing about it. One former aide imagined these headlines which would have been written about him: **'*Michael Jackson Considering Suicide*',**

'Social Services Take Away Jacko's Children', 'Jacko in a Prison Burst Up'. He continued: *"Michael's death was also a blessing in disguise for the tabloids".* And when I asked why? He pointed out that the days following his death, British tabloids which included the defunct *News of the World* and its sister paper *The Sun* recorded sales of more than 1.5 million copies between them in less than one week. In America, *The Washington Post* and *National Enquirer* also sold more copies in the week Michael Jackson died than they normally did before his death. Electronic media and web-based channels experienced dramatic increase in viewership and download while some of them suffered outage. Such was the pulling power of the late King of Pop for newspaper readership which was the one of the main reasons why the world media pursued him every where he went and speculated in every thing he did. Although Michael Jackson was a very beneficial brand to the media, irrespective of that they castigated and ridiculed him until his last days.While the media tore him apart, some members of his family exploited the situation as they wanted to use the willing press to promote their own agenda too. One of the family members who came out with gun blazing in all direction in 1993 when Michael had problems was his sister LaToya. Out of anger or jealousy, LaToya appeared on TV in 1993 in the full view of the world to destroy her brother and that was at a time when his brother was most vulnerable and would have needed her support. Ironically on Michael's death, LaToya was the first one to run to his house to take inventory of items.

The major ethnic groups in America had mixed feelings about Michael Jackson. The black people accepted him as one of their own but were disappointed that he went to mess his skin colour and change his facial appearance, the Hispanics liked his music but resented him as he was not one of their own while the white people liked his music as too but had difficulty dealing with his various accusations of child abuse. Sensing all the above, the American media saw good opportunity to continuously savage him without any opposition. As for the British press, their main aim was to exploit his name and image to increase newspaper sales. In order to entice British readers, some of their tabloids came out with these sensational headlines about him:*'Explosive Jacko Files', 'Jacko Bombshell Tape', 'Riddle of Wacko Jacko Family', 'Jacko Picked up Love Child in Hotel', 'Jacko Horror', 'Jacko's Jab to Curb Sex Urges for Young Boys.'* And if there were any British tabloids that took Michael Jackson stories to a whole new level, it was the ones owned by Rupert Murdoch. The other tabloids from America to Britain contributed in no small way to Jackson's frustration and depression which was one of the reasons why he became dependent on powerful drugs to ease his nerve and the pain he was suffering in his heart. He eventually died from overdose. But after his death, the media quickly washed their hands off the whole saga and instead labeled him a 'drug addict'- a terminology which resonates well with the public because drug abuse is mostly associated with celebrities.

The media claim to serve a plural society and expose the ills of society but in reality they are more concerned with profit.Tabloids in particular have no morals. They don't see anything wrong with publishing stories stolen from mobile telephones of unsuspecting individuals or images obtained by harassment by the paparazzis. *News of the World* in Britain in those days was in the forefront of encouraging the above type of practices.The opportunism of the British tabloids aside, studies have shown that British people, more than any other people are the most sexually repressed and avid voyeurs in the world and this has made them become heavy consumers of gossip, titillating news and sensationalism. The attitude of the British people is one of the reasons why tabloid journalism has continued to thrive in Britain. Up and down the country, people have directly or indirectly continued to support rogue tabloids because they buy what ever nonsense the tabloids publish.

In Britain they once had the king of sensationalism and his name is Max Clifford. Over the years, Clifford made a lot of money from peddling sensationalism to the tabloids. Although he never handled or sold any stories concerning Michael Jackson to the tabloids but sex stories similar to the type that plagued Jackson was his exclusive domain. He thrived on celebrities' misfortunes by selling stories of their sex escapades, etc to the media. However, in 2013, nemesis caught up with him because Mr Clifford forgot the adage which says: Don't throw stones if you live in a glass house. I remember watching him on TV whenever there was *BREAKING NEWS* about a celebrity, including an interview he gave about Michael Jackson when he died in 2009. Selling sensational sex stories to the tabloids in those days, Max Clifford became a millionaire. While Rupert Murdoch's tabloids *The Sun* and the defunct *News of the World* dug the grave, Max Clifford provided the corpses that were buried in them. In the year, when Jimmy Saville scandal broke out, Clifford was approached by the media to give his opinion. As he was talking about the late Mr Saville on TV, he did not realize that he was digging his own grave! Talk about hypocrisy! As he was on TV slaughtering Saville, some women he had abused when they were young saw him and quickly made reports to the police about their own respective cases with him in the past. In 2014 Max Clifford was found guilty of child abuse and jailed for eight years. While one of his clients in those days-*News of the World* was also exposed for the fraud it was for the criminal tapping of peoples' mobile telephones earlier in 2011 and was shut down for good. The cool PR mogul who collaborated with many tabloids in Britain to ruin peoples' lives will now live out the rest of his life as a convicted paedophile. What goes around comes around.

The world was in awe of Michael Jackson but the white media establishment was also jealous of him. In their opinion, Jackson was a black man who was too big for his shoes. The media pretended to praise him at some occasions but inwardly they hated him and found it difficult to tolerate his success. They figured out that something had to be done to curtail his influence and if possible, arrest his success. The white media would often seek out anyone who was prepared to come up with any sensational or damaging story about Michael Jackson. They didn't need to verify any story they picked up about him. Once it is Michael Jackson, any news about him would sell. The establishment and the white media's plan were to negatively influence people's opinion about Michael Jackson. And they succeeded in doing so.

During the Gavin Arvizo case, the LAPD sent an unprecedented 70 police officers to search Michael's home known as *Neverland*. The idea was to dramatise the arrest and brand him also a fugitive who indulged in molesting children. Meanwhile Tom Sneddon who was the the chief police officer prosecuting, wanted to be the star. In the process of searching Michael's home and arresting him, Tom Sneddon displayed a very high degree of arrogance. Whilst announcing Jackson's arrest on the 18th November 2003, Sneddon huffed and puffed in front of several microphones and announced that Michael Jackson was a *'WANTED MAN'* and that he should hand himself over to the County Police Force as soon as possible. Now remember that Michael Jackson was a household name in America and all over the world and would have no place to hide like a petty criminal. Nevertheless the police poked fun at him and declared him 'WANTED'. When a reporter asked if the LAPD had contacted Michael or his people before calling a press conference for his arrest, Sneddon's answer was riddled with mockery: *"Michael Jackson should get over here and get checked in"* to the delight and amusement of his audience. Sneddon's answer was disrespectful to Michael Jackson and he purposely wanted to tantalise millions of viewers who were in front of their TV at home to watch the humiliation of one of the greatest entertainers in the world. In the continued mockery of the situation and of Jackson in particular, some members of the press even asked Sneddon to provide them with lunch, drawing more laughter from the audience. To answer to their request, the police told the pressmen that they should be able to increase the sales of their newspaper from the Michael Jackson story and afterwards make donations to help proscute him.To finish off the press conference, Tom Sneddon issued a warning to parents: *"DO NOT ALLOW YOUR CHILDREN TO GO TO NEVERLAND OR GET NEAR TO MICHAEL JACKSON".*

Enter CNN.The news channel immediately gathered some analysts in their studio to start analysing Michael's arrest.The anchor on that day, Kyra Phillips was revelling in the situation and limelight which Michael Jackson's arrest brought on to the news wave. Phillips was flanked by a blonde lady and a court 'expert' who in spite of not knowing Michael and his family personally, started making some remarks about the Jacksons. As I listened to Ms Phillips and her guest, I immediately came to the conclusion that their 'expert' analysis was nothing more than speculation at best. I also personally felt that their opinion boiled down to condemning Michael as guilty already. As I zapped through other news channels in America and Britain, I noticed that all of them were almost indirectly pronoucing Michael Jackson guilty. But all of the people who thought Michael would be jailed might have eaten their words later as after five months of the trial, came the verdict.

On the day of the verdict, the whole world was glued to their TV set and I in particular was zapping from one station to the other before finally settling once again with CNN. On the day of the judgement, I noticed a different anchor, this time Nancy Grace and her team who were once again almost predicting a guilty verdict for Michael Jackson. Soon I got bored with their analysis and decided to move on to other channels. Surprisingly what I heard was not different to the opinions that were been expressed on CNN. Finally I decided to hang on with CNN. As the world waited, the court martial came out and began one by one to disappoint all those who were wishing that Michael was thrown in jail. Michael Jackson was one by one pronounced innocent on all counts and was acquitted from the crime he was accused of by gold diggers and their supporting LAPD and media establishment.

From when he was a young man and with Jackson 5, Michael Jackson was aware that the sole aim of tabloid newspapers and magazines are to make money at the expense of celebrities like him. He also knew that accuracy, fairness and truthfulness did not matter to the media as they are in a cut throat and competitive business. Guided by his fear of the media, he more or less shunned journalists except when it was absolutely necessary to talk about his music. After the Jody Chandler saga, Michael actually completely cut off media access to himself and his house hold. And the staff members that worked for him at the time were also made to sign an agreement that forbade them from talking to the media. After 1993, it took Michael Jackson 10 years to grant an interview to a journalist and that was to Martin Bashir in 2003. Of course the media did not appreciate the invincibility of a mega star whose stories could earn them plenty of money but they waited to see Michael's next move. While the cat and mouse game between him and the media continued, Michael began privately to put together a plan to tour the world again. However, he figured out that in order to connect to the people once again, he must rebuild his image after the saga of Jody Chandler and that the best way to do it was to make a documentary that would portray him as a friendly and charitable person, especially with regard to sick children.

Enter Martin Bashir a Pakistani-born British journalist. Michael, I am told saw the documentary the journalist made about his friend, Princess Diana who was having problem with her husband shortly after their marriage. In order to seek sympathy from the British public, Diana agreed to allow Martin Bashir to interview her so that she could tell her side of the story. The project was hugely successful in favour of Princess Diana. In the meantime,

Martin Bashir made his name with the documentary. So when Bashir contacted Michael Jackson to do same with him as he did for Princess Diana, Michael fell for the opportunity without thinking it through. According to my sources, *"had Martin Bashir not interviewed Princess Diana before she died, he (Bashir) would not have had the chance in a million years to get close to Michael Jackson, what more to make an opportunistic documentary about him. In giving permission and access to Bashir to come into his life Michael let his guard down and ruined himself forever"*. Bashir's powerful closing statement in the Jackson documentary captivated and shocked the public and drew the attention of the LAPD, an organisation that was looking for another opportunity to continue their 'unfinished work' on Michael Jackson from the time of Jody Chandler in 1993. When Michael was alive, he knew and understood that a mega star like him would attract public attention but what he could not accept was the brutal lynching of him in order to sell newspapers and films, the sort Martin Bashir made about him. He was very distressed by the published part-truths and sensation-grabbing stories of the tabloids. He said tabloids print part of a story that will grab headlines and leave the part, which is the actual story that would not sound sensational.

In the case of tabloid newspapers, their stories are in most cases devoid of any real news content. They choose sensational front page headlines and brand them *exclusive* in order to ensure maximum circulation and sale of their newspapers. Michael Jackson was the tabloids' perfect choice of a celebrity because they know that they will sell whatever they printed about him. Aside from celebrities however, the tabloids also dealt with anybody or any story they consider shocking enough for the public. *Abuse* and *Rape* stories even when they are not substantiated are still good for the tabloids because they use such stories to embellish their papers. In a few words, the tabloids have the morals of the devil.

In England one of the factors that brought down the

News of the World, was the fact that the rogue tabloid continued for about a week to publish stories about a dead teenager. Although the newspaper was aware that a young girl had tragically lost her life in the woods they continued to hack personal information from her mobile telephone and were publishing the texts as 'exclusive news'. The tabloid was later caught out about the crime. The criminal ways which were used in obtaining information for most of their news in those days forced *News of the World* to close down in 2011. Some of their journalists were jailed and or cautioned for the crimes of entrapping celebrities and tapping peoples' telephone. A certain Mr Mazhar Mahmood who worked for the *News of the World* and was hailed as one of the best undercover journalists and a bastion of excellent journalism by her boss Rebekah Brooks was investigated for perjury and entrapment in 2014. Mr Mahmood's case related to the entrapment of the singer Tulisa Contostavlos whom he said was dealing in drugs. But Mahmood was later exposed as a liar and manipulator who among other things, spiked drinks to entrap his victims. According to Ms Contostavlos' lawyer, Mahmood entrapped celebrities, bent the truth and invented sources to create "*big-time, glamorous stories which enhanced his reputation and that of the The Sun on Sunday and its predecessor News of the World.* Meanwhile, Rebekah Brooks, who was the managing editor of Mahmood and other journalists who were hacking private individuals' phone system in those days in order to make *News of the World* look special, got off free.

Reading a tabloid newspaper is like shoving your head into a rubbish bin. After the merest glimmer of hope that you may have discovered something special, you are encouraged to look deeper. But after a while you realise that what you have actually found is rubbish covered with smelly baked beans and cold tea bags. It is only then you realize that you have just wasted your precious time looking for a pie in the sky. Tabloids are 'voyeurs' and their owners are only interested in making money from peoples' private lives. Tabloids recognize that today's public has voyeuristic tendencies and they exploit this opportunity to the fullest. Tabloids write about celebrities as if they are some sort of super human beings or folk heroes. It is in the interest of the tabloids to create this illusion about celebrities in order to tantalise readers to buy their newspapers.

Jackson family and the AEG

Following Michael Jackson's death, his family took his last promoter, AEG, to court. But they lost the case and it is not difficult to see why. First of all, Michael Jackson was an adult when he entered into a contract with AEG to perform in London in 2009. He was also an accomplished musician and had been in the business for more than four decades. He was aware of all the pros and cons of signing a contract to perform in a live show.

He might have been vulnerable at the time because he was struggling with poor health which nobody knew any thing about including AEG. Michael was also said to be in financial difficulties at the time which might have forced him to agree to perform 50 gigs in one week. Before AEG approached Michael Jackson, he had been living a reclusive life and had distanced himself from his family. He had also gone to live in the Middle East for a while after he was acquitted from the Garvin Avizo case in 2004. When he returned to America two years later he continued to live a reclusive life with only his young children as companions. At that time, he was no longer living at his splendid home *Neverland* and had moved to live in a rented villa in the outskirts of LA. He was also said to be short of money. In fact when Michael died in 2009, it was reported that his credit card was worth almost nothing. No one knew that Michael was poor in health and had no money too to continue living the opulent life he was used to in the past 40 years. As I am told, at that time also when when he returned back to America from the

Middle East, most of his high paid advisers had left him. So when he signed with AEG he was more or less on his own. *"At that time Michael had only a few professional staff and hardly any strong adviser in his team so he took most of the major decisions on his own"*, a close staff member told me. Signing with AEG to perform 50 concerts for a frail 50 year old man was a huge decision. It was a decision which unfortunately cost him his life because he intensified the use of Propofol and Demerol to help him sleep so that he could engage in the rehearsals he needed for the London concert. Unfortunately it became a concert he did not live to perform.

One can understand the pain of a mother who lost her beloved and precious child. Katherine Jackson was heartbroken by the death of Michael and wanted to find out the circumstances which led to her son's death. But taking AEG to court over the death of her son was a big mistake. As for the opportunistic media agencies who wanted to shape public opinion about the cause of Michael's death, it was easy to want to link AEG and Dr Murray to the causes of Michael's death as the two were the last organisation and individual respectively who were in contact and or involved with Michael shortly before his death. The Jackson family might have been influenced by what they read in the newspapers and decided then to sue AEG. I am told by reliable sources close to the Jackson family that Katherine was warned by some members of the family not to sue AEG but she still went ahead. As predicted she lost the case. My source continued: *"If the Jackson family wanted to be angry with anyone or some people for the death of their son and brother, they should have directed their anger to the gold diggers, paparazzis and the rogue media organizations that hounded Michael throughout his life and even on his death."* His brother Marlon indirectly addressed individuals and media organizations who chased Michael almost to his death when he knelt beside his brother's corpse and said to him *"Michael, now that you have gone, may be they will leave you alone."*

Before his death on 25 June 2009, Michael Jackson might as well be described as a dead man walking. The powerful drugs which were administered to him by Dr Conrad Murray may have finished him off but the truth was that Michael was before he fnally died, a broken man. He had no friends, had some how deserted his family and was running out of money. He wasn't eating properly and his health was detoriating faster than any one imagined. He lived a reclusive life and was very much withdrawn from the world. He interacted only with his children and domestic staff. Although his family had long suspected that something was not right with him but he hid his drug use, problems and frustrations from them and everyone else. Because of the child molestation accusations he had passed through and many other legal cases which were connected to different claims, Michael at that time was described to me as an angry man on the inside. He was also paranoid and was skeptical of people including members of his family. He didn't want to meet anybody.

Before his troubles, Michael was almost the sole bread winner of the Jackson family; he provided for his parents and others in the family in every way he could. And to the outside world including the media, his name and image were a source of making money especially, for the celebrity intoxicated tabloids. Everybody wanted a piece of Michael Jackson. This affected him badly and his health spiralled downhill. While his popularity waned, the media continued their harassment; shocking and spiteful stories about him were published every other week if not daily. The irony was that most of the things published were hearsay presented as facts. An American journalist Diane Dimond published a book in 2005 about Michael Jackson which was heavily based on hearsay and innuendo. Bob Jones, who worked as PR man for Michael also published a book which was more of revenge after Jackson sacked him. Other journalists including JaneVelez Mitchell and Maureen Orth also published stories which held strong anti-Jackson bias.

Some years before Michael passed away, it is not an overstatement to say that he faced a group of individual writers and white media organisations which together with the establishment were bent on having a go at him. It is also correct to say that before his death in 2009, there was a negative campaign of Michael Jackson which amounted to a calculated lynching exercise. In England during the week he died, the tabloids took up the habit of referring to him as ***'Weird Jacko', 'Dopey Jacko', 'Wacko Jacko'*** and ***'Knackered Jacko'*** among other references of him. By the time these derogatory refrences were reprinted and or read in other countries, the negative impression of Michael Jackson was already stuck in peoples' psych. During the live coverage of his death by many news organizations, analysis of his life was mixed with portraying him as a paedophile even though no court EVER found him guilty of such a crime. During his death, many TV presenters took their turn to have a go at him. In a post Michael death interview, Diane Sawyer wondered what Lisa Marie Presley was doing with him. She asked her *"Micheal Jackson, what about the way he looks?"* Barbara Walters who moderated Martin Bashir documentary on Michael Jackson took her own barbed shots at him with some critical comments.

Michael Jackson got into show business from a very young age. When he was only 5 years old he was already the lead singer of the family band, Jackson 5. The Jackson family used their influence in those days to establish a private talent show competition in their neighbourhood of Encino, California. Judges for the Jacksons' talent show included the family partriach Joseph and young Michael. Among the families who took part in the Jackson's talent show in those days was a certain Ronald Newt family. His children, Ronald Jnr and Robert, were talented but still amateurish. Ronald Snr envisaged that his boys would need some professional coaching so he contacted the Jacksons for help. After watching them perform, Michael and his father were impressed and agreed to take them under their wing. The Newts were invited to move in with the Jacksons at their Encino mansion where they would undergo some serious makeover before taking them out to perform in public. Young Michael was tasked with coaching the Newt boys while Joseph Jackson became their manager and promoter. One of Joseph's immediate actions was to get the Newtons as they were known in those days to perform a gig at the popular Roxy Club in West Hollywood. Michael, as their coach, went over to see The Newtons' first show. The Newtons did well on their first show. Joseph Jackson's next move was to land the boys' a recording contract and supervised the production and release of their first two albums. After this good start, the boys faded into oblivion. One would expect that that was the end of the Newts family. But 20 years later in 1993 when Michael Jackson got into trouble with the Jordy Chandler scandal, America's number one tabloid magazine *National Enquirer* desperate for a scoop and any story that might link Michael Jackson to be nailed as a paedophile, went out of their way to fish out Ronald Newt Snr and his family. The editor of *National Enquirer* at the time, David Perel, drew up a contract and offered the Newt family $200,000 to go on record and claim that Michael was sexually involved with his children Ronald Jnr and his brother Robert when they were hanging out with Michael in the 1970s. Jim Mitteager a reporter with *National Enquirer* was given the task of getting Ronald Newt to sign the contract. A meeting between the latter and Jim Mitteager took place at the Marriot Hotel in downtown San Francisco. But Ronald Newt Snr, after a thoughtful consideration, knowing fully well also that nothing inappropriate happened between Michael Jackson and his children had a change of heart and declined the offer from *National Enquirer*. In the meantime, the magazine had drafted a news headline which was to be published the next day to support the fact that Michael Jackson was a paedophile from long time ago.

The above shows how tabloids will go to any length to frame a famous celebrity in order to increase newspaper sales. It is an open secret that tabloids sometimes pay out huge sums of money to frame a celebrity or politician in order to obtain their so called *'exclusives'*. And when it is not possible to frame somebody, some journalists working for tabloids would entrap celebrities by spiking their drink in order to confuse the victim and obtain 'forced' admission or confession of something the victim didn't do. Mahzar Mahmood of the defunct *News of the World* was a master of this type of snare.

While Michael Jackson ignored many things that were written or broadcast about him, nevertheless he did take action in some 'exclusives' that bordered purely on lies. For example in 1995, he authorized a $100 million dollars lawsuit against journalist Victor Gutirrez, a freelance journalist who was at the time based at Vernice Beach, California. Other individuals and organizations that were named in the suit included Diane Dimond and her Los Angeles radio station KABC-AM, Paramount Pictures, Roger Berkley, Ken Minyard and Stephen Doran. The case was connected to an alleged video which was said to contain footage of Michael Jackson having sex with a 13 year old boy in the shower who was actually his nephew, Jeremy Jackson, Jermaine's son. Victor Gutierrez was said to have exclusively acquired the video entitled HARD COPY. In a statement from Michael Jackson at that time that accompanied the case, he said *"There have been vicious lies and rumours about a video tape of a sexual encounter between I and a 13 year old boy. I will no longer stand by and watch reckless members of the media try to destroy my reputation. I intend to protect myself and my family. I have instructed my attorneys to immediately file lawsuits against those persons who continue to spread vicious lies and rumours about me in their attempts to make money, benefit their careers and sell papers or to get viewers to watch their programmes."* After court deliberations, it was found that the alleged tape did not exist and if there was any tape of that sort, it was a fake. The court ruled that the allegation was false and malicious and awarded Michael Jackson $2.7 million in damages. Diane Dimond was luckily spared by the court but the architect of the news and false tape, Victor Gutierrez, filed for bankruptcy and ran away to Mexico.

To improve viewership, I was told that in 2003, NBC allegedly offered Michael Jackson $5 million dollars to go on air and be quizzed about Gavin Arvizo. Michael, I am told, took the offer as an insult and entrapment and of course turned it down. NBC denied the allegation at the. In the fight for ratings, mainstream radio and TV channels were always ready to pay big money to a megastar like Michael Jackson to go on air and be interviewed.

The Paparazzi

Paparazzi work is an underground industry which is not regulated. Activities of the paparazzi endanger lives and yet politicians on both sides of the Atlantic have failed to take any action against the illegal activities of these men and women with lenses who go around harassing people. Perhaps it is a case of robbing Peter to pay Paul as some of the politicians and so called celebrities owe their rise and much of their popularity to the paparazzi.The proliferation and profitability of tabloids and gossip websites in the last 2 decades have also given rise to paparazzi activities.

Tabloids and gossip websites are in competition and in order to outwit each other, have figured out that they need to embellish their stories with photographs and videos clips. Although most media organizations may have in-house photographers but their employed photo-journalists may not be able or be in a position to obtain photos and video clips that may be necessary to support a story or what they consider as hot news. So the tabloids therefore resort to using freelance photographers popularly known as paparazzis to obtain exclusive photos and images of celebrities, sports men and women, politicians and even of private individuals which will support a hot story. Not to be left out, other mainstream newspapers and TV stations including online websites have also joined the tabloids in paying large sums of money to paparazzis to buy photos and images of unsuspecting victims which in most cases would have been obtained illegally. As most celebrities, politicians and private individuals may not be willingly to give permission to paparazzis to take photos of them and their family to be splashed accros the pages of tabloid and mainstream newspapers, paparazzis have resorted to obtaining such photos and videos by often hiding by the corner or bushes around their target's homes and take photographs or record videos of them illegally. Since it is a celebrity mad society, any photos or video clips of stars such as the late Michael Jackson and Princess Diana were worth hundreds, if not thousands of money. Tabloids in America, England and other western countries have funds already set aside to acquire paparazzi photos and images which would help to embellish any story they are writing about a celebrity. Therefore, the market for paparazzis to sell their criminally obtained images is always there. In a tacit connivance with individuals and to widen their network of information, paparazzis also use accomplices such as butlers, airline staff, waiters, car park attendants, night club bouncers and personal chauffeurs who will give them information of the movement or lifestyle of their bosses. In return for their information the accomplices would receive a percentage of the paparazzis fee when the latter sell the information and or images he or she has obtained from the tip off of accomplices.

Michael Jackson on many occasions was a victim of these types of set up. During Jody Chandler and Gavin Arvizo cases, a number of Michael Jackson staff members were approached by the paparazzi and tabloids to sell their stories and or images of Michael Jackson which they may have in their possession.While some declined, others sold out.

Diego Maradona, the Argentine football legend who is

no stranger to conflict once decided to teach the paparazzi a lesson. On one fateful day in August 2014, Maradona went to the cinema with his young son. It was an outing which he had promised his son and which he wanted to keep as a family day. But a certain paparazzi who wanted to cash in on the event and take photographs of father and son to sell to the tabloids got into trouble with Maradona. The paparazzi had been stalking the Maradonas for many hours and when the star noticed him, he gently told the paparazzi to back off. He said to him *"This outing is a gift for my child. One of the first days I have had time to spend with my son after the World Cup. I want a quiet environment with my young son, so stop following us please. And by the way, I am 53 years old and my name is Diego Armando Maradona not Dieguito"*. But after several warnings, the paparazzi did not leave the family alone. Then Maradona got fed up, exited his car and asked the paparazzi: *"What is is it you want? Why mess with my family if I don't mess with yours?"* Maradona then landed a slap on the face of the stalker and drove off. Mike Tyson and Russell Brand have respectively also given the paparazzi a taste of their own medicine. I remember Tyson once knocked one of them out! Since politicians and the courts are not interested in protecting individuals from paparazzi harrasment, more people might be tempted to take it unto themselves to stop the paparazzis from harassing them and their families. During his golden years Michael employed very strong and tough bodyguards, but I am told that he advised them not to handle the paparazzi with heavy hand.

Although in different circumstances, it is easy to compare the paparazzis role in making Michael Jackson unhappy to the role they played in the death of Princess Diana and Dody Al Fayed in Paris in 1997. It was the media which encouraged paparazzis to continue to chase Diana and her boyfriend wherever they went in order to obtain photographs of the two together. Paparazzis last pursuit of Princess Diana and Dody Al Fayed resulted in the terrible car crash under an overhead bridge in Paris on August 31st 1997 which killed them. Just like Jackson's death, while there was outrage in the circumstances that led to the death of Princess Diana and Dody Al Fayed, the British media quickly washed their hands and shifted the blame to Dody and Diana's driver whom they said was drunk. The British public however, bought the media's version. Why? Well, because to the British people, it was an abomination for a royalty as Princess Diana, to be dating an Arab and a Muslim man.

Enter TMZ, the brash online gossip media. The web based channel based in California, USA does obtain most of its information from the paparazzi. TMZ was actually the first channel to break the news of Michael Jackson's death in the early hours of 25 July 2009. Nevertheless, TMZ is also the sort of media organization which encourages the infestation of the paparazzi in the society. TMZ 'reporters' some of whom may better be described as paparazzi themselves would often walk around Hollywood during the day stalking celebrities all over the town. And later on in the evening would gather in their California studios to discuss and disect and broadcast news of talentless people such as the Kardashians, Paris Hilton et al. TMZ 'reporters' makes one wonder if some people have actually decided to become wasted potential.

CHAPTER SEVEN

MICHAEL JACKSON AND WOMEN

The memorable days of Jackson 5 included the fun the brothers had with lots of women. Jackson 5 was the hottest boy band in America in those days and their popularity stretched to other parts of the world. Their brand of music, Afro haircut and fashion style, which included colourful and garish stage costumes, captured the attention of women worldwide. Initially it was mostly black youths in America who followed the band but with the release of *I Want You Back* and *ABC* both of which went on to reach No1 in America and England the white youths joined the Jackson 5 bandwagon. Women,usually the most passionate fans of musicians, were always available and some of the elder Jackson brothers did not allow opportunities of hooking up with beautiful women pass them by in those days.When any of the Jackson brothers wanted a woman, they never had any problem picking up one. Although all five brothers had their different attributes in music and physical appearance, Michael was however, considered the cutest and as he was the lead singer with a velvet and silky voice that could melt a woman's heart, he was the one most women wanted to meet. But in those days he was still very young between 5-15 years old and quite shy. History has it that he never really got involved with women in those days nevertheless he became the carrier of messages between women fans and his elder brothers.

It is no secret that women are impressed by fame, wealth and power. A man who has any one of the above would easily be attracted to lots of women and would probably be spoilt with choice. From when he was with Jackson 5 and witnessed what went on between his brothers and women, Michael later as an adult became wary and cautious of women. During the days of Jackson 5, women would mob the brothers wherever they went. At their live concerts it was always difficult to control the mob of hysterical women who wanted autographs and photos while others wanted to touch, hug and kiss the brothers. Michael was terrified by the mob of girls who wanted to touch, hug and kiss him while performing on stage and or when he and his brothers step out to go shopping privately. He said later as an adult that he knew that the girls didn't mean any harm but that they were still rather rough. He said he has marks and scratches on his hands and could remember from which city he got each mark. Those times were very scary experiences for young Michael. Girls inflicting physical damage on him were some of the reasons he became a bit skeptical about women in his adulthood. He also recalled that the wildest mob scene he ever saw was in England. From America, heading for a concert in 1972, over the Atlantic the pilot announced that he had just been told that there were ten thousand people (most of them women) waiting at Heathrow Airport for the Jacksons. To Michael, the announcement was exhilarating but at the same time very threatening. He recalled that the Jacksons were lucky to make it out of the airport alive.

Although he loved women and did not mind interacting with them but when it came to love and serious relationships, *Michael was very sceptical of women and even confused as to how to handle them. He was also deeply concerned that most women are vain and wanted a relationship with him because he was Michael Jackson.* One of his former staff members told me. As Michael became more famous in later years, the negative perception of women got the better of him. For some reasons he was very cautious of dating. He was also concerned that with the kiss and tell culture that became the hallmark of the 21st century tabloid press, the intention of some women who wanted to date him was because they wanted to be close to him so that they could have some information about him which they would then sell to the media. Irrespective of his worries however, after he left the family house in Encino to live on his own, Michael did date a few selected women. He was careful however to choose women who were mature, had their own fame and name to protect, from well known families and or those who like him, grew up as child stars. His reasoning was that the type of women as described above would understand and commiserate with him and would not be tempted to sell the story of their relationship to the media.

I was told that although he dated some women in his teenage days but shy Michael was in all likelyhood not sexually involved with them until later in his adulthood. No doubt, Michael loved women but his fear of their intention towards him, coupled with his introvert nature, never allowed him to fulfil what is really expected of man-woman relationship. He found it difficult to trust women and this lack of trust got worse as he grew older, richer and more famous. He was not sure if women wanted to be with him because he was one of the guys or because he was a superstar. He felt his relationships were disappointing, had concerns with trust and felt that girls probed too deeply to try to work him out. He said that some of the girls he dated tried to use sexual relations to attempt to control him; all of the above he found difficult to accept about women.

Irrespective of his reservations however, Michael dated some smart and decent women. His first *'real'* date was Tatum O'Neal, the step daughter of Farah Fawcett, the famous 1960s actress who incidentally died same week as Michael, in June 2009. In his private diary, Michael indicated that Tatum O'Neal was his *'first love'*. He wrote that they spent a lot of time together and attended several high profile parties, including some at the mansion of Hugh Hefner, founder of *Playboy* magazine. However, Michael said also that Diana Ross was actually his first love. But as those close to him told me, it is confusing to know what he meant by saying that Diana was his *'first love'*. No one knows the true story behind Michael's continued proclamation of Diana Ross as his first love. Was their relationship intimate? Diana Ross was pivotal in the development and promotion of Jackson 5 and the boys lived with her in California before the Jacksons eventually bought their family home at Encino. I was told that Michael was closer to Diana than any of his brothers. It is said that even after the Jacksons left her house, Michael was a constant visitor to Diana's house and also became her companion to many events. After many years the Jackson brothers left Diana's house and Michael went solo, he still would visit Diana regularly and went out with her hand-in-hand to many of his invites and vice versa. But true to his introvert nature Michael bottled up his emotions about Diana but would become very jealous whenever Diana was with another man. When she eventually married, although he was delighted for her, another part of him was jealous as he said that he actually really loved Diana. But why was Michael hurt that Diana Ross got married to another man? Did he assume that Diana was his 'lover' in an emotional way? How deep did he think their relationship was? Until his death, Michael never revealed the extent of their relationship at least, from his own personal perspective neither has Diana confirmed or denied the meaning of the 'love' Michael was proclaiming for her. My sources told me that Michael was a young man who was probably infatuated with Diana Ross and that there was no sex involved in their relationship. Having said that, whatever happened between the two of them has remained a closely guarded secret which Michael took to his grave.

Another one of Michael Jackson's former lovers was Brooke Shields, the young actress of the *Blue Lagoon* fame. Michael in his writings, confirmed that they were *"romantically serious"*. Brooke Shields went on several dates with him and was his confirmed girlfriend on and off for a period of time at least until 1993, as reliable sources informed me. Brooke Shields, like Michael Jackson was also a child star. A few years yonger than Michael, she was quiet, smart, pretty and was raised in a stable family. Brooke was not the type of woman who would kiss and tell, so Michael felt comfortable in her company. It is believed that their relationship was on and off until it slowly fizzled out some years later, about 1993. However, Michael and Brooke Shield remained best of friend right up to his death. She turned up at her best friend's funeral ceremony at the Staples Centre in Carlifonia in 2009 to give a heart-wrenching eulogy.

Madonna was another star who is believed to have briefly dated Michael Jackson. They attended a number of functions, spent some private time together and *'surveyed'* each other's body while in the privacy of Michael's home, but as Michael noted in his personal writing, Madonna was not his type of woman. What brought them together was that at that time, the two were the biggest 'A' list celebrities in California and felt that it was cool for the two biggest stars in town to be seen together at events. As is well known and Michael being aware of it, Madonna is a very loud person the complete opposite of Michael. Needless to say, their companionship did not last for more than a few outings.

Enter Elizabeth Taylor. She was a friend and mature acquaintance of Michael Jackson. Both of them professed that they loved each other. Michael used to spend a lot of time at Elizabeth's place and they also passed nights at each other's homes. They went out on dates and held hands as close friends and lovers do. Michael said that Elizabeth Taylor would often feed him like a baby whilst in bed. She was also his sole confidant and would discuss many important and personal issues with her. However, the level of their relationship was never also made clear by either of them before they both died. Michael never wrote or said much about his relationship with Elizabeth Taylor.

Other women who were in Michael's life included the late actress Katherine Hepburn, with whom he shared intimate dinners and passed the night at each other's place. Liza Minelli is another Hollywood star Michael mentioned in his private writings. The two dined and drank together whilst singing and trying out various dance moves at each others home. Michael wrote that he had one of the best times with Liza Minelli and that he loved her very much.

A close study of the women Michael went out to dinner with or dated shows that he preferred mature and rich women including the women who were already celebrities in their own right. Michael Jackson was very protective of his private life and the last thing he wanted was to have stories of his relationships splashed all over the papers. He figured out that mature women who were also rich and famous like himself or those who were from well-known or rich families would never be interested in discussing their relationship in public or sell their stories to the media. He avoided women he didn't know their background.

Michael was also a late starter with women and was rather timid on how to handle serious relationship and this was hampered by the fact that he was also a very shy man. Seeing Michael gyrate on stage and clutching his balls, one may not realize how shy he was but put Michael to speak on one on one to an individual, one would notice how he covers his mouth when he smiles and put his face down if asked a question such as love relationship and sex. He was also his own worst critic whether it was about his music, dancing and or his physical appearance. I gathered that one of the reasons why Michael prefered the company of teenagers and mature women was because he felt comfortable with them as opposed to those he thinks want get into his head and or ask him some serious personal questions. He believed that young teenagers and older women were the last people who would judge or critique him or the way he looks.

In 1994, shortly after marrying Lisa Marie Presley, Michael went with his new wife to visit Donald Trump, the American estate mogul in New York. Although he was the guest of Trump and stayed for a few days at his penthouse, in the same building where Trump lived but Trump later said that he saw Michael only once in a week while he was staying at his place. The singer and his wife had locked themselves up in the penthouse they were assigned for days without seeing or talking to any one. Micheal later said that concealing a little bit of him from people is a way of getting some much needed space. He felt strongly about the lack of privacy in his life and hiding himself away like he did at Trump's place and at various other times during his life, gave him some respite.

Apart from the women mentioned above, I have also been told that outside public and media glare, Michael quietly and privately had flings with some of the most beautiful women one could imagine. They were not escorts as Dr Murray claimed after Jackson died but respectable women whom Michael had thoroughly vetted. Some of the women I am told would be sneaked into Michael's private quaters and would spend time with him and leave quietly afterwards. His closest staff members were warned never to divulge any news about the women who visited him. It is said that only one or two of his trusted staff members would arrange such a meeting. Did Michael have sex with them then, I asked? *"Of course he may have done"* my sources told me. Michael totally respected the many fabulous women who entered and shared his life, especially those not in the public eye, and would not disclose their details to the media because of his views on privacy.

It is obvious that women like to throw themselves at male celebrities and rich men. My advice would be for the man to go for it. But before doing so make sure the woman you are going to sleep with sign a legal document and possibily film the encounter which would absolve you from any claim whatsoever later which might include abuse and rape. Once this is done, then go on and have lot of fun with women, especially with women who are celebrity hunters.That is what people like Mike Tyson and Tiger wood should have done! It is hypocritical to read that some women who are adults would on purpose and without being forced, throw themselves at celebrities and afterwards cry rape! Many elebrities have paid a heavy price in their unguarded romance with women. It is to be noted that no woman ever made any serious sexual claim against Michael Jackson.

Ironically no beautiful woman goes to the media to say that she had been forced to have sex with a homeless or a very poor man. First, the story would not be of any news value to the tabloids, secondly it will not be sensational enough for the gullible and voyeuristic public to buy such a story because it is not connected to a celebrity. But if the claim is about Tiger Woods, Eddie Murphy, David Beckham, John Terry, Silvio Berlusconi or Mick Jagger, then the tabloids and even mainstream media would have a field day writing about it. Women know that they have incredible sexual power and they use it to control, manipulate and exploit men. For those who claim rape or abuse, if the law courts don't give them what they want, they call the defunct *News of the World* which was the first choice in those days or *The Sun, Sun on Sunday, Daily Mirror or Daily Star* in England and if in America, they call the *National Enquirer*. Michael Jackson's mistrust of women including the media and the LAPD inspired him to write the song *Leave Me Alone*.

Not long ago, a woman's desire and natural instinct would be to start a family with a man and her sex drive was also uncomplicated. Some time ago too, a woman's priority was to seek security for herself and her future offspring by looking to meet a real man with whom she could settle down and produce children. This natural instinct of the female specie could also be found in wild animals. Female animals in the wild instinctively look out for strong males with whom they would mate in order to produce a future generation. There is nothing wrong with this animal instinct. But the 21st century woman has taken the survival instinct to a whole new level! What we see today are some women who are masters of deceit and who want to sleep with a celebrity in order to entrap him and make money from the liaison. The pages of tabloids in the past three decades have been filled with kiss and tell stories, broken relationships and high end divorces which have been sold to the tabloids by women who have dated celebrities and high profile sports men. To titillate the public who are also voyeurs, the tabloids would brand the stories they have acquired as *'exclusive'* in order to sell their newspapers.

Michael Jackson was well aware of the entrapment culture used by modern women; he was scared of it and so decided to shun the women of whom he was not sure of their background. I am told that had it not been for the kiss and tell culture of the 21st century, Michael might have had a normal relationship with a woman with whom he could have produced natural children. He told some of his trusted staff that he could not openly have a girlfriend adding that he did not think that he would ever be totally happy if he had to have a permanent girlfriend because the media would do everything possible to destroy the relationship.

Lisa Marie Presley

Michael's dream was to start a family and have his natural children who would carry on his musical gene and continue his legacy. He reasoned that if he married a woman who had music flowing in her blood like he had himself, their offspring would naturally excel in music and entertainment. From Michael's private writings, he gave the impression that his choice of woman whom he would like to have as mother to his future children would be of caucusian descent. Without any prejudice to his black race, Michael's wish was aslo to have light-skinned children. *"Although he never said anything of this sort openly but I have the impression that Michael wanted light skinned children to reflect his light skin appearance after plastic surgery. I believe that he wanted also to erase in his mind, the teases he received from his father as an 'ugly' and flat nose boy"* a former staff member told me. Coupled with the above reasons, Michael also wished to have a woman who was brought up in a good family, have a famous family name like he has and if possible have a wealthy background too. He wanted his children to have both worlds. And if a woman with the attributes as above decide to marry him, he hoped it would be for love and not because he is Michael Jackson.

It's no surprise therefore that his first wife Lisa Marie Presley matched all the qualities as above. Lisa Marie is the daughter of the late King of Rock and Roll, Elvis Presley. Lisa Marie ticked all the boxes as the ideal woman and wife who would become the mother of Michael's future children. *"Michael couldn't have made a better choice of a woman who matched his wishes"* my sources told me. Lisa Marie's background was as solid as Michael's. She was born into a family of fame and wealth. She was also very well raised by her mother Priscilla. Lisa Marie was not some sort of a cheap woman who wanted to get close to Michael in order to prop up her own rise to celebrity, fame and or use him to make money by selling her story to the media afterwards should any thing happen between them. Lisa Marie is rich in her own right, as the only heir to her late father's estate. *"Michael was also confident that Lisa Marie would never go public about their relationship. Ok she did some interviews after their marriage ended and after Michael passed away but she never did it for money neither did she divulge any sensational details about their relationship"* My source said.

Michael was aware of the protective wall which was built around Lisa Marie by her mother, Priscilla and he appreciated her demeanour and attention to detail. After his troubles with Jody Chandler's family and the LAPD in 1993, Lisa Marie was one of the people who rushed to comfort him. Michael and Lisa Marie spoke a lot in those days and confided in each other. Michael trusted her very much and they would spend hours talking on telephone. Before 1993, he had met Lisa Marie in the company of her father in California. They had earlier also exchanged telephone numbers but rarely spoke with each other prior to his child sex accusation in 1993. But after he settled the case with the Chandler family, Lisa Marie became one of the persons he frequently spoke to and shared problems with while at same time seeking advice from her. With time, their friendship grew and progressed to a loving relationship. Having dated for just a couple of months, on the 26th of May 1994, Michael and Lisa Marie secretly flew to the Dominican Republic where without informing any of their families got married.There were no family members from either side or large group of friends present at the wedding, only a handful of individuals who acted as witnesses. For some reason which he never disclosed, Michael believed that his family, especially his mother Katherine, would not approve of his marriage to Lisa Marie and therefore never bothered to tell her and or any member of his family before tying the knot with her. On the other hand too, Lisa Marie also suspected that her mother Priscilla would likely oppose her marriage to Michael, so decided not tell her either. In the Dominican Republic, a local pastor married them without any fanfare. Afterwards from their hotel room, Michael called his mother to inform her of his marriage to Lisa Marie Presley. But Lisa Marie's mother Priscilla only got to know that her daughter had gotten married to Michael Jackson when she turned on the TV the next morning to listen to the normal daily news. Then 'Breaking News' flashed through her TV screen: ***Michael Jackson marries Lisa Marie Presley***. At first Priscilla never believed what she had just seen over the airwaves but her fear was confirmed when she saw helicopters hover around her estate with paparazzis on board, waiting to catch a glimpse of the newly married couple coming or going from the Estate. Of course Michael and Lisa Marie were no where to be see because bride and groom were still in the Caribbean and their families back in America did not even know what the two had done! Reliably sources told me that Michael and his inner circle had meticulously planned the marriage to avoid any huge publicity which the wedding of a mega star like him would have drawn had he notified a large number of people in advance. With the marriage to Lisa Marie concluded, Michael's next thought was to begin the planning of a family with children in tow.

Contrary to what was printed in the newspapers and magazines in those days, a reliable source close to Michael told me: *"Michael and Lisa Marie's marriage was consumated. Sex between them was great and more than anything else, Michael wanted to start living again and start a family. He wanted to put the Chandler issue behind him. He would spend hours in bed with his new wife, playing around and confiding in her. Michael felt he had found a trusted person for once"*. Before he went out fully with Lisa Marie and married her, Michael was very skeptical about meeting people including members of his Jackson family. Although he didn't have lot of old friends but those who wanted to become his new friends or music associates for that matter were very much vetted. The problem, I am told was that he actually trusted nobody. To make matters worse, after his sister LaToya went on TV in 1993 to denounce him during the Jody Chandler saga he became suspicious of everybody including his Jackson siblings. Some people close to him said that at the time he married Lisa Marie, he was a bit of an 'angry man'. He was angry at the media, he was angry at some members of his family and he was angry at some of his ex-staff members who had sold stories to the media when he had problem with Jody Chandler family. All the above combined with his childhood which he felt he lost during his time with Jackson 5 also made him a bit of a frustrated man. But as he was finally married to the woman of his dreams, he wanted to concentrate on his new wife and together plan for children. He didn't want any distraction and for this reason basically cut off communication from the world including members of his family, apart from occasionally speaking to his mother Katherine.

Michael Jackson was born into a big family. Growing up with many brothers and sisters influenced him to think also that he could one day have a large family too. He planned to marry, have children and even dreamt of having a very large family (13 children) with the right woman. And he meant it. After all, with his wealth at that time, raising 13 children would not have been any problem as it was with his parents who with their meagre income raised 9 children. *"I can't resist babies"* he told the press after visiting a childrens' hospital while touring Japan in 1987. With his marriage to Lisa Marie Presley, Michael also wanted to prove to the world that he was no child molester and by starting a family with her would also show his detractors that he was a caring and family oriented man who simply enjoys the company of children.

Unfortunately as problems began to crop up with their marriage, encouraged also by Pricilla refusing to approve of the marriage, Lisa Marie held back from becoming pregnant for Michael. But what Michael Jackson also didn't take into account was that Lisa Marie had been married in the past and has 2 children from her previous marriage. So she was more experienced than him in the ups and downs of marriage. She was also worried about the fall out on their their future children should their marriage collapse. Although she loved Michael but she was also concerned about his eccentric behaviour. And most importantly, as her mother Priscilla did not approve of her marriage to Michael, she wasn't sure if she could continue in the union. It was no secret that Priscilla never liked that Michael married her daughter and was of the opinion that the singer married Lisa Marie just for image purposes. Pricilla believed that her daughter was tricked into the marriage so that Micheal would use it to restore his shattered reputation after the accusation that he sexually molested Jody Chandler in 1993. In her own words, she was *"concerned and suspicious"* and thought that Michael had an '*'agenda''*. Mrs Presley never gave up putting pressure on her daughter to get out of the marriage. I was told that LisaMarie with time did actually fall inlove with Michael and wanted their marriage to work but her mother's pressure coupled with her own worries about Michael's eccentricity bothered her to no end.

Priscilla's pressure was one thing but her daughter was also very concerned about Michael's behaviour such as his continued application of beauty makeup when at home and in bed, his erratic and snappy behaviour at times and his obsession with having teenagers come around to sleep over at their mansion. Lisa Marie was fed up soon after the marriage and was already confused.Then after living together for just a couple of months, she also got a first hand opportunity to notice that Michael, although being one of the most eligible and richest bachelors in the world at that time, was a '*wounded*' young man. His lost childhood, accusation of child abuse, bad experience with the media, the police and gold diggers had made Michael a bruised man. She couldn't comprehend how she was going to live a happy life with a man who seemed frustrated on all fronts. All the above led her to begin to have second thoughts about the marriage. She was worried and wondered how they would raise children under those circumstances. After their divorce in 1995, she said this of Michael: *"He was like a young boy, angry at the world. Who hasn't had a miserable childhood?"*.

As regards Michael's love of hanging out with teenage boys, she knew it was actually much to do with him trying to reclaim his lost childhood but she also wished that her husband scaled down the number of young children who were always visiting their home to sleep over. I was told that on several occasions, she would remind him of the trouble he got himself into with Jody Chandler in 1993 and pleaded with him to cut back his interaction with young boys. But Michael did not listen. Sitting beside him once during a television interview, Lisa Marie was shocked to hear Michael confirm that he would continue to ask young boys to come over to *Neverland*, where they lived at the time time to sleepover. Lisa Marie after that interview seriously began to wonder if she had done the right thing by marrying Michael Jackson. Although there was sex in the early part of the marriage but that faded with time. The irony was that Michael wanted to have children but Lisa Marie told him: *"I think we have to have sex in order for me to get pregnant but we are not doing it."* As time passed, it became evident that their marriage was not working. In the meantime, both of them decided to keep cool about any plans of having children. The idea of abandoning their plans for children was good for her anyway because she was actually worried that should children be involved in their marriage and if they were to divorce, the custody battle would end up becoming one of the most talked about celebrity break up of all time. And she did not want that to happen.

Although Michael Jackson had his side of the problems which might have prompted his wife to seriously doubt that their marriage would work, Lisa Marie on her part had the tendency to pull out of a relationship quickly if she thought it was not working. It must be pointed out that Lisa Marie never had any money issue with Michael during their divorce and has since after divorcing him married for the 4th time and is now settled down. But a philosopher once said that marriage is for peasants and not for the rich. The narrative is that the chance of two poor people sticking it out in marriage is far greater than two rich people doing so. Poor people most time cannot afford the legal bill and the money involved in divorce, so they have no choice but to stick it out. For the rich people, money is not a problem to settle a divorce hence they will not hesitate to sort it out as quickly as possible and move on. Philosophically speaking then, while 'romance' is for the aristocrats 'love' is for peasants.

Lisa Marie is a rich woman in her own right. Her father, Elvis, was a megastar, became an institution after his death and left his only daughter load of money which includes an estate in Tennessee which is also a money-making facility. Lisa Marie does not need any man's money and can call any man's bluff any time. As her marriage to Michael Jackson was not working it was not difficult to accept a quick and amicable divorce without any monentary conditions and move on. Moreover, there were no children involved so there was really nothing to fight for from both side. So after agreeing to go their separate ways without demanding anything from each other, their divorce was officially granted on the 18th January 1996. After divorcing Michael Jackson, in the same year, Lisa Marie got engaged to John Oszajca but broke it off after a few months to hook up with the actor Nicholas Cage. She married the latter in August1996 but again ended it just 4 months later. She has since married her fourth husband. With money you really can call any man's bluff! Although it is easy to understand Lisa Marie's concern and reasons for not bearing children for Michael Jackson however, had she done so, she would have become the proudest mum in the world today because their children would have carried Michael's and Elvis' genes and in all likely would start what could be a coveted Presley-Jackson music dynasty, because blood don't lie.

Debbie Rowe, Prince, Paris and Blanket

Debbie Rowe was born into a rich family. She grew up on her parents' ranch just outside California. During her youth, Debbie mingled with hippie young men. She rode motor bikes with boys and wore black leather trousers and jackets. As is usually the case with young and middle-aged white bikers, Debbie drank beer and tequila. Although she had rich parents she was always broke and lived with other young men and women in rented apartments in her rural California community. But irrespective of her hippy lifestyle, Debbie Rowe took studies seriously and successfully qualified as a nurse. After graduating from the nursing academy, she moved to Los Angeles where she took up job as a nurse and receptionist in the clinic of celebrity dermatologist and skin cancer physician Dr Arnold Klein. Elizabeth Taylor, one of the high profile Hollywood celebrities at that time was a client of Dr Klein.

She was also a close friend of Michael Jackson. It was Elizabeth Taylor who recommended and introduced Michael Jackson To Dr Klein.

During adoloscence, Michael developed skin problem which was diagnosed as vitiligo. His skin disorder worried him and greatly affected his life. Between the ages of 10 and 24, he was already a superstar and an 'A' listcelebrity. Fans and every other celebrity in Hollywood at that time wanted to meet and take photographs with Michael Jackson. But the mega star who every body was talking about had one big personal problem. His face was covered in pimples! During his teen years Michael was constantly plagued with pimples and rashes which would cover most of his lower body, part of his neck and face. Unbeknown to many people and in spite of his wealth and popularity at that time, Michael was the unhappiest young man in Hollywood. Each morning he would spend hours in his room examining his body. As if the pimples were not enough, he also began to take a dislike to his nose, his thick curly black hair and the general state of his white cum black patchy skin. Michael's most fervent wish then was to appear 'immaculate' to his fans and Hollywood friends. As a big star, appearance meant everything in Hollywood in those days and still does till this day.

The lifestyle, image and appearance in Hollywood of celebrities were and still is, all too tempting to follow and not easy to ignore especially if one is in the public eye. As Michael was growing up and becoming the peoples' man, the thought of changing his appearance to follow the trend in Hollywood was not something he could resist. It was also about this time that he recalled how his father used to tease him about his Negroid features. He once told an audience that in the early days when he was growing up and acting naughty, that his father in a bid to get back at him, would tease and call him the boy with the *'big, flat nose'*. He also said that Joseph would often jokingly refer to him as the *'ugly one'*. Could it then be that his father's teases contributed to making Michael become insecure with his natural Negroid appearance? One cannot say for sure. But what was certain was that inspite of the confidence he radiated on stage Michael, as he was maturing into adulthood, began to hate his natural physical appearance and was hell bent in transforming himself with the hope that it would give him more confidence and attract more white audience to him. He had also seen how some celebrities in Hollywood in those days transformed their looks from plastic surgery and went on TV to brag about it. In fact in the 1980s, Hollywood exploded into a land of 'plastic dolls', a place where men and women who looked like extraterrestrial creatures could be seen trotting all around town. Elizabeth Taylor, Judy Garland, Joan Collins and many others have all done plastic surgery, some of them multiple times. Michael Jackson was part of the 'A' list celebrities in Hollywood at that time and he didn't see any reason why he shouldn't join his peers with a new look. So with the advice and recommendation of his close friend Elizabeth Taylor, Michael went over to see Dr Arnold Klein. The singer wanted a new appearance to match those of other Hollywood stars with whom he was friends. Afterwards he defended his surgery publically by insisting that a lot of famous people have had surgeries and that plastic surgery is long recognised and widespread in Hollywood. He said that he has only had his nose altered twice and added a cleft to his chin. But he did not mention that he had also undergone medical procedure to remove the white patches that was developing all over his body because of vitigo.

From puberty, Michael suffered from a skin condition called vitiligo which is a skin disease of black and albino patches appearing on someone's skin. Granted that he had vitiligo but it seems the disease also gave him the perfect opportunity to do away with the old *'ugly'* Michael as he said his father used to call him. A former staff member told me in confidence that *"Michael was terrified of getting old. His wish was to look young forever and he thought that plastic surgery would do it for him. But he was also an artist and felt that twicking his appearance would be be a good thing for his entertainment business"* When he started his second round of surgeries including whitening his skin at Dr Klein's clinic, he was divorced from Lisa Marie Presley and was on *"a mission to transform himself and start a new life. He was also desperate at that time to have children as he always loved children"* I was told by a former staff member. After Elizabeth Taylor introduced Michael to Dr Arnold Klein in the spring of 1996, Michael quickly formed a close friendship with the doctor. Their friendship as revealed in the latter part of this book was to change the course of Michael's life and future generation forever.

Prior to moving to Hollywood in mid 1996 to work, Debbie Rowe was a young woman who was more of a tomboy than a flashy 90s girl. She came from a good family who lived in the rural valleys of California. As is the case with young people in their early teens, she was some sort of a 'rebel'. Whilst living the hippie life in rural California, Debbie never forgot that she needed to upgrade her education and credit to her, she proceeded to qualify as a nurse. After graduating from the nursing school, she moved to Hollywood to seek for new opportunities in her profession. She joined the clinic of Dr Klein as a receptionist-cum-nurse. It was at this clinic that Debbie met Michael Jackson in the autumn of 1996. Whilst he received treatment there, Debbie became Michael's personal nurse and carer. She put in tremendous effort to care for Michael when he was admitted at Dr Klein's clinic and during his regular visit as well to the clinic after he was discharged. Michael instantly liked Debbie Rowe for her care and the personal attention she gave to him. They became good friends and would talk about many things. After sensing that Debbie is a true professional, calm and a good listener, Michael, unusually for him, loosened up and began to confide in her.

He told her how he did not trust many people because he had been let down many times and that because of his bad experiences with some people he had trusted in the past, including some members of his family, he rarely had any more close friends. Meanwhile Debbie, a completely changed person from her hippie days, surprised Michael with her down to earth approach and answers to some of the questions Michael would pose to her. Debbie's calm nature and understanding made Michael believe that he had found someone he could talk to in confidence. He was also surprised that a woman who was not related or involved in show business or part of the celebrity circle in Hollywood would captivate him in such a manner.

With Debbie's training as a nurse, Michael also noticed that after several months of attending Dr Klein's clinic word did not leak out to the media that he was using the clinic for his medical problem. Michael liked that kind of privacy. He appreciated that Debbie was a true professional who upheld the ethics of her profession. He began to take a liking on his nurse. While Ms Rowe listened and comforted Michael on his many troubles, more than anything else, she never disclosed their friendship to anyone. Michael was very much impressed about Debbie's attitude. Needless to say, on her part, she liked Michael as well. Although she was his nurse but she had also followed his music and was his fan as well. Irrespective of his status as a mega star whose medical news would be of interest to the media, Debbie Rowe kept Michael's medical condition and record confidential. More importantly also, she was a member of staff at Michael's best friend's clinic and could not jeopardise her job and profession by selling Michael Jackson's story to the media.

As pointed out earlier, one of Michael's desires when he married Lisa Marie Presley was to have children with her but as their marriage collapsed earlier than any one expected, he waited for some time to launch another plan of having children. Debbie Rowe might not have been in his league and was not a celebrity by any stretch of imagination but she matched most of the requirements as well for the type of woman Michael wanted as an 'ideal mother' for his future children. Debbie is Caucasian, blonde, mature and level headed. She was also his personal nurse and knew first hand of all the medical problems he was having, including his vitiligo and the recurrent pain from the burns he suffered some years back when he was filming a Pepsi Cola advert. So as he felt comfortable with her he immediately decided not to let the opportunity of a nice and respectable woman who would bear his future children, pass by. After assuring himself of Ms Rowe's qualities, his next move was to discuss it with his friend Dr Klein. He told Dr Klein that although he doesn't love her in that sense but that he would want Debbie to bear him children as a surrogate mother. Dr Klein immediately acquiesced to Michael's idea. So after the two agreed and discussed it with Ms Rowe, a plan was hatched for her to be artificially inseminated with a male sperm so that she could become surrogate mother for Michael's first child. As pointed out earlier, Michael might not have been sexually attracted to Debbie but he saw her as an ideal surrogate mother to bear him children. On her part, and as expected, Debbie could not turn down Michael's request, afterall at that time he was one of the world's most eligible bachelors and a superstar.

After agreeing on the necessary conditions, Debbie Rowe was inseminated with a male sperm, which until this day no one knows who the donor of the sperm was but as a result, she became pregnant and 9 months later gave birth to Prince. After one year, Debbie was inseminated for the second time with another male sperm for the conception of his second child Paris; once again the identity of the donor is not known till this day. However, since Michael's death and as the faces and appearance of Prince and Paris have been revealed, questions have started to be asked as to who is the natural father of the children because the two children have have no resemblance whatsoever to their father's ancestry. While their father is of Negroid descent, the two children are of pure Caucasians. While some people have suggested that the two children bear unquestionable resemblance to Dr Klein, the true answer of who their natural father is will be something the world will continue to wonder for a long time. A reliable source close to Michael told me unequivocally that Michael never had sex with Debbie but he wanted a close friend whom he trusted to donate the sperm for his children *"He liked Debbie Rowe for her openness, simplicity and understanding and she liked him as well but as their friendship grew, she also realized that Michael did not fancy her for sex. She was made aware and fully agreed that she would only be a surrogate mother for his children"* My source said.

After Debbie Rowe became pregnant the first time with inseminated sperm, Michael was very happy that he was going to become a father. But there was one drawback. Michael and his family are members of the Jehovah Witness Faith. In view of his religion and public image, he did not think it was right to have children out of wedlock. Already pregnant with Prince, Debbie and Michael flew to Australia and on the 14th of November 1996, got married there. The private ceremony was held at the Hilton Hotel in Sydney and only an eight year old boy was present as his bestman. The marriage was also held to placate Michael's mother Katherine whom Michael held in very high esteem. One of Michael's staff who travelled with them to Australia told me that *"after their marriage, husband and wife retired to separate rooms to sleep."*

A lot has been said and written about Michael's relationship with Debbie Rowe and their two children Prince and Paris.While some of the rumours could not be substantiated, one thing is clear, Prince and Paris, God bless them, do not seem remotely to have Michael's blood and genes. The truth also is that their appearance, do not in any shape or form bear any resemblance to Michael's Afro-Negroid heritage. So much so that when Michael died in 2009, some Caucasian men came forward to claim that they donated the sperm for the conception of the two children. While all the bogus claims could be put aside as opportunistic from men who wanted publicity and or money from the Jackson estate, the grapevine has it that the most likely donor of the sperm for the two children is Dr Arnold Klein. Since Michael's death, Dr Klein has neither confirmed nor denied the rumour! And as Prince is growing up and to a lesser extent his sister Paris, it is not an overstatement to say that their physical resemblance to the physician is extremely striking. For Michael and Debbie as was probably planned, after their 'marriage arrangement' ran its course, Michael Jackson and Debbie Rowe went their separate ways in November 1999. It is said that Debbie Rowe was paid $4.2 million to sign off on the custody of Prince and Paris. Michael kept and was raising the children before his tragic death in 2009. Meanwhile, Debbie Rowe has since returned to a private and quiet life in her rural California.

Michael looked forward to having many children as he himself came from a big family. After Prince and Paris were born, true to his word of having a big family, Michael went on to have a third child called Prince Michael 2nd- aka Blanket. He was born on 21 February 2002 through artificial insemination as well by a surrogate mother whose descent is believed to be of Latin America. The world may suspect Dr Arnold Klein to be the sperm donor of Prince and Paris and we all know that their mother is Debbie Rowe but nobody can say whether it was Michael or another man that donated the sperm for his third child, Blanket. Neither does anyone know the identity of his mother. Looking at Blanket grow up however, one may notice that he has some traits of Michael in his features but it is still difficult to say for sure if he was the biological father of his youngest son. One impressive thing though is that in spite of Michael being a superstar from whom it is easy to make money by selling any story about him, Blanket's mother, that is, if she ever knew the father of the baby she was carrying for 9 months was Michael Jackson, has kept her silence till this day and has never come out to tell the world that she is the mother of Blanket. Credit to her, one must say-amazing.

As said earlier, among Michael Jackson's 3 children, the one that has some physical resemblance to him is Blanket. As he continues to develop, his true genetic identity will become apparent and time will tell if he will be the one who will eventually step into his father's shoes. For all my love of Michael Jackson and his children, I regret to say that the King of Pop made a big mistake in deciding that the best way to have his children was by artificial insemination of surrogate mothers and with the sperm of other men too. Among other questions left unanswered before his passing and probably the most intriguing one, is why the most famous bachelor in the world at that time decided to make children by artificial means. Granted, he did not trust women because of the fear of selling out but at least, he should have chosen a woman, vett her very well and have normal sex with her; perhaps obtain some legal assurances from her not to sell her story to the media for a period of time and make children with her. And if he didn't want to have natural sex with any woman, then at least, use his natural sperm to inseminate a surrogate mother. Having sperm donated by other men for his children was to me one of the most weirdest things Michael Jackson did. With his action, what he ended up doing was to directly or indirectly encourage some fellows who went to the media after his death in 2009 to claim that they were the donors of the sperm for his children! Irrespective of the above, all indications however, point to the fact that he did not leave his DNA behind with all its inherent talent to continue the next generation of Michael Jackson.

Meanwhile, some of the opportunists who went to the media to claim that they were the natural father of Prince and Paris include a certain Mark Lester and Matt Fides, both from England. After their initial claim however, every thing went quiet from their end respectively. Dr Arnold Klein, who is the best person believed to know who donated the sperm for the children went to court in

America to seek for protection against any inquiry to that effect. He said that while he was not prepared to discuss the donors of the sperm, the well being of the children is the most important thing to him. Rightly so, one would say too. As to those who claimed they were the donors of the sperm for Prince and Paris Jackson respectively, I say to them, while there are millions of poor and orphaned children in America and Britain begging for recognition, none of you went to the newspapers to claim paternity of those poor children? Why must it be the children of Michael Jackson?

As to why Michael decided to use surrogate mothers for his children, an insider told me, *"After Lisa Marie left him, Michael was very sad and depressed. He had in mind that Lisa Marie was the ideal woman with whom he could have sex and produce natural children. However, as they divorced before children could come along, Michael became angry, confused and frustrated. As he was always sceptical about having serious relationships with women and yet wanted to have children, the decision to have an unknown woman who is not a fan or a celebrity to bear children for him was probably the best solution. Debbie Rowe who is the mother of Prince and Paris and the unknown mother of Blanket were his options."*

Of course, Michael Jackson's three children are lovely. And they all seem to possess the grace and elegance of their late father. Prince, Paris and Blanket meant everything to their father and he was raising them to the best of his ability before he tragically passed away. Until his death in 2009, the world did not know what Michael's children looked like. When he took them out in public he would cover their faces with veil. One theory was that Michael was temporarily trying to shield himself from questions of who might have fathered the children as they do not look anything like children from a mixed parentage. But upon his death, the Jackson family decided to do away with the veils and masks and the world then saw the true identity of Prince, Paris and Blanket. It was after their faces were revealed that every one realized that something did not quite match as there is no trace of black ancestry or mixed one in the children at all. What we know now however, is that although Michael was a black man, his children are completely caucasians. For those who might want to enter into a debate, children of a mixed race would at least draw something from either of their parents, no matter how little or remote. But in the case of Michael's three children, there is no trace of black features or heritage whatsoever in three of them. This is not to say that Prince, Paris and Blanket are not Michael's children. Far from it, he was the father they knew from infancy and was raising them before he tragically passed away.

Michael was a very private person and he went about making his children in the most secretive way ever. Their heritage apart, the question is will Michael Jackson's children follow in their father's footstep as an accomplished musician and entertainer? I for one don't think it will happen. First of all, their father was and would continue to be a very tough act to follow or copy. Secondly, the truth is that Prince, Paris and Blanket do not carry Michael Jackson's DNA. And since the genetic hereditary is not in them, I would argue that they can never replicate one atom of Michael's talent. Having said that, if any of his children eventually become as good as he was in show business, it will only be because they were partially raised by the genius himself and have also subsequently continued their development under a family that have music in their blood. Whatever, it is difficult to see how this will happen. I understand that for emotional reasons, some people including Michael's fans and family may disagree and or deny this fact but this is the truth of the matter. Before he died, Michael had wished that his children would follow in his footsteps but I am not sure he thought about the proverb 'like father, like son' when he was 'making' them through artificial means. I have mixed children myself and am sure many of us know what a mixed child look like.

So despite my love for Michael, it breaks my heart to say that Michael Jackson did not leave his DNA behind so that his legacy will be naturally preserved.

CHAPTER EIGHT

MICHAEL JACKSON AND OPRAH WINFREY

With all the pomp and pageantry associated with Michael Jackson, he was actually never comfortable giving interviews or appearing on talk shows. In those days, before Oprah's interview, hundreds of journalists would on a daily basis approach Michael's management with request for interviews but almost all of them would be refused. Oprah Winfrey's interview with Micheal was held on the 10th February 1993 at his *Neverland* ranch home in Santa Ynez Valley, California. Oprah's interview was granted after 14 years of not giving any interview to any journalist or news organization! In that interview, Michael spoke about his lifestyle, eating habits and the skin problem-vitiligo which he said had been bothering him for many years but had hidden it from the public. Oprah Winfrey's interview of Michael Jackson was watched by more than 90 million Americans and over 200 million people worldwide.

Before the interview, Oprah Winfrey was simply another show host who was not well known in America at that time. But after Jackson's interview, Oprah's status rose like a meteorite and her subsequent shows also saw a dramatic rise in viewership. The interview turned out to become a career changing opportunity for her. While the interview in many respects benefitted Oprah Winfrey and shot her to stardom, it kick-started the fuss about Joseph Jackson being labelled as an abusive father. In Oprah's interview, Michael hinted that he and his brothers had a strict upbringing with their father who was always on guard to make sure they did not go down the wrong path when they were growing up in Gary, Indiana. However, that honest assessment of his father's strong approach in their upbringing was twisted to give the impression that Joseph Jackson abused his children. While Michael never used the word 'abuse', Oprah's questions and presentation tactics implied that Joseph was an abusive father. That set in motion the tabloids frenzied serialization of Michael Jackson being abused by his father when he was growing up. Aside from the above however, Oprah's derogatory question about Michael's vitiligo such as *"you don't like being black"*, also led to public cynicism about Michael's skin condition.

Michael granted Oprah Winfrey a no-holds barred interview with the aim of showing his fans how he lived at his home *Neverland* which is located in the Ynez Valley of California. At that time, Michael was a very elusive person but with Oprah, he was willing to open himself up before the global audience. So he did not set any rules for the questions and did not insist on any contractual conditions that would have protected him from been misquoted or miscontrued. For the interview he simply wanted to be natural in order to give the audience a glimpse of how he lived privately. Michael didn't need any media publicity when he granted Oprah Winfrey the interview, rather it was the other way round because any media person who had the opportunity then to interview Michael Jackson was on the way to becoming a celebrity.

Oprah Winfrey became what she is today, partly and greatly, thanks to Michael Jackson.

CHAPTER NINE

MICHAEL JACKSON vs MARTIN BASHIR

"I trusted him to come into my life and that of my family"

-*Michael Jackson*

If there was any organization, news agency or an individual that caused grave damage to Michael Jackson, no one matched the harm done by Martin Bashir. Talk about the last straw that broke the camel's back. Martin Bashir was the guy who finally put Michael Jackson on his knees. The Pakistani-descent British journalist, who after gaining Michael's confidence, travelled and lived with him and his children for many months as he was making a documentary on them, was responsible for the damage of Michael Jackson and his brand before his death in 2009. Reliable sources told me that the decision by Michael to allow Martin Bashir, a complete stranger to walk into his personal life was a mistake he regretted very much and which haunted him until the day he passed away.

Prior to meeting Michael Jackson, Martin Bashir had produced a number of documentaries for the British Broadcasting Corporation (BBC). He had also conducted high profile interviews of some celebrities and politicians in Britain. But the documentary that put Bashir's name on the world stage was his 1993 Panorama documentary of Princess Diana, the late ex-wife of Prince Charles. Diana was the darling of the British people and during the period of her marriage to Prince Charles the English public was fascinated by her and the stories of her marriage to the Prince. The English nation was ever ready to consume anything that was broadcast or published about Princess Diana. Diana's elegance and style of fashion including her devotion to charitable causes captivated the British people.

Diana in a few words was the peoples' princess and doing a documentary about her life was bound to be successful and well received. The stories of her problematic marriage to her ex-husband Prince Charles were also of interest to the people and would often be the best *'exclusive'* gossip of the British tabloids. In those days, any news about Diana, Charles and the English royal family were always a sell out and still is till this day. Martin Bashir intelligently seized the opportunity of the British peoples' hunger for sensationalism, especially when it is about their royal family to produce a documentary about Princess Diana. Like Michael Jackson in music and entertainment, Diana was the star of the royal family and both were celebrities whose stories would sell newspapers and increase TV viewership in those days. Martin Bashir had the foresight to capitalize on the advantage and approached Princess Diana for a documentary which would inform the British people of the problems she was going through in her marriage. The documentary which presented Diana as a neglected wife and the victim of a marriage that wasn't working due to Prince Charles infidelity, stole the heart of the British people.The documentary was also presented in such a way that it pitched Diana against Prince Charles and the rest of the royal family. After the documentary was broadcast, opinion polls showed that the clear 'winner' was Princess Diana.

After it aired in Britain and won lot of reviews and accolade, the documentary was shown in some American TV channels. Michael Jackson being a good friend of Diana at the time took an interest and watched it too. As the documentary became worldwide phenomenon, Martin Bashir saw his status rise as an investigative journalist. He instantly became the media man every celebrity or politician wanted to hire to portray him or her in a good light. A celebrity journalist overnight, Bashir felt he had conquered Britain so his next move was to be America. Subject: the biggest star in town. Person of interest: Michael Jackson.

Princess Diana met Michael Jackson a couple of times before her death. Their first meeting was when Michael performed in London on 16 July 1988. During the meeting which took place in the green room before Michael went on stage, they exchanged pleasantries, gifts and telephone numbers. On returning to America, Michael would, from time to time, call Diana late at night. Their conversation would last several hours into the night and they would talk about many things, including their celebrity life and the pressure associated with it. When Diana's documentary was broadcast in England and America in early 1993, Michael watched it and like every one else thought that Bashir did a great job of presenting Diana as the victim of an 'arranged' marriage. He also thought that the documentary portrayed Diana in a very good light before the British public. Michael took notice of the producer who was Martin Bashir. And his staff also briefed him that the Diana documentary raised the image of the Princess in a very positive manner in Britain. In 1993 shortly after Diana's documentary was broadcast, Michael was accused of sexually molesting Jody Chandler. Although he settled the case privately by paying off the Chandlers with $200,000 million dollars, his image was dented by the scandal. So when Bashir approached him 10 years later to shoot a documentary as he did for Diana, Michael realising that he needed to do something about his dented image, accepted the offer. Meanwhile, in 10 years since Jody Chandler's case, the singer had married Lisa Marie Presley and although the marriage did not last long but 2 years after divorcing Lisa Marie, he married Debbie Rowe who became surrogate mother to his 2 children. About the time Bashir contacted Michael, he was already planning a new European tour. America might have been hostile to him after the Chandler scandal but Europe, particularly England, always loved Michael Jackson. So if there was to be any revival of the King of Pop, Europe was the ideal continent to start the mission.

Apart from the promotional and publicity activities

already lined up by Michael's management team for the European tour in 2002, any other promotion of him and his music business was obviously to be welcomed. So when Martin Bashir contacted Michael to shoot a documentary about him as he did for Princess Diana, the singer did not hesitate to agree to the project. The idea was that Bashir would join the singer and his entourage to travel around Europe and film his tour while at same time capture some private moments of him, his children and teenage friends who visited him at his *Neverland* home after each segment of the tour. The main idea of the documentary was to show to people a 'new Michael Jackson' whilst hoping that the documentary will help restore his battered image after the Jody Chandler scandal. To shoot the documentary, Martin Bashir lived with Michael Jackson at his *Neverland* ranch home in California for six months. He also travelled extensively with him in America and joined the singer in his European tour. During their travels, Bashir was allowed to film freely as Michael and his team believed that he was the ideal journalist who will present him in a positive manner and help to change the negative perception people held of him after he was accused of child molestation in 1993. In the meantime, having been carried away by the euphoria of Bashir'swork, Michael overlooked signing a contract which would give him the right to approve the contents of the documentary before it is broadcast.

The documentary entitled *Living with Michael Jackson* which took six months to shoot, was released and broadcast worldwide on the 3rd February 2003 without Michael been made aware of some segments of the documentary especially Bashir's closing statement. The result of this oversight turned out to be that Michael Jackson had unintentionally collaborated in a documentary which triggered the chain of events which completely wrecked him. Over the years, Michael Jackson had suffered a severe burnt accident, freed himself from the first accusation of child molestation, divorced his first and second wives and was dependent on anesthetic drugs to help him steady his nerves and sleep but Bashir's documentary which was supposed to show Michael in a positive image ended up becoming the project which finally wrecked him. According to one of his closest staff *"that documentary 'killed him' before his actual death 5 years later"*.

The opening part of the documentary started well but progressed to a shocking conclusion during which Bashir announced that he was greatly *"disturbed by Michael's relationship with young boys"*. To buttress his argument, he cited one of the segments of the documentary where Jackson was filmed holding hands with Gavin Arvizo and the boy resting his head on Michael's shoulder. Gavin was one of the young friends of Michael and a regular visitor to *Neverland* at the time.

Gavin Arvizo was 13 years old and was suffering from terminal cancer during the time Bashir made the documentary. Michael met Gavin during one of his regular visits to a children's hospital in down town California. He became friends with the boy and his entire family. The Arvizo family would often be invited to *Neverland* during which the whole family would spend time with Michael and sometime pass the night at *Neverland*. On the day in question, when Michael was talking to Bashir on camera Gavin was spending the weekend at *Neverland* together with other children. As part of the documentary and answering to Bashir's question about how he lives and his charity work, Michael told him that he would often play with the children who visited him and that some of them also slept over at his place with the permission of their parents. During the interview on camera, Michael was sitting with Gavin, holding hands with the boy and Gavin resting his head on Michael's shoulder. Little did Michael realize that his comments and his sitting arrangement with Gavin would be misconstrued.Then after editing the documentary and in a final analysis of the film, Bashir seized that moment of Michael and Gavin sitting together to announce that he was greatly disturbed by Michael's relationship with young boys! Bashir's closing statement of being deeply *"disturbed"* by Jackson's friendship with teenage boys and his, Bashir's body language suggested that he might have seen or suspected that something inappropriate was happening between Michael and his young friends. As expected, the documentary raised eyebrows and got people talking. The LAPD which had been trailing Jackson since he got free from the Jody Chandler allegation in 1993 (the outcome of which they were not happy with at the time) seized Bashir's documentary and the closing statement to set in motion the revival of the case against Michael Jackson as a child abuser. Before Bashir's documentary, the LAPD had felt for quite sometime that Michael had short-changed them by 'buying out' Jody Chandler's family with a $22 million pay off in 1993. Now with Bashir's new documentary, the table has turned and there was enough evidence to open a fresh case against him. In the opinion of the LAPD at the time, Michael Jackson has now been caught red-handed indulging in inappropriate behavior with an under-age boy.The 'concrete evidence' to prosecute him which Tom Sneddon, the LAPD officer in charge at that time had been looking for since 1993 had presented itself on a plate of gold!

Before the trouble of Gavin Arvizo, Michael felt he had to do the Bashir's documentary because he wanted to dispel the notion that he was a paedophile, an accusation which has been bordering him since Jody Chandler in 1993. But it backfired. His trust and naivety in agreeing to do the documentary brought him disastrous consequences and damaged his reputation beyond repair. Michael later regretted doing it but it was too late. He agonised about it to the very last day he died. *"After the documentary was broadcast, he was heartbroken and never recovered from the shock and the consequences, including the damage to his person, fame and the huge amount of money he spent fighting the case.The stress of all that led him to increase his dependency on Demerol and Propofol which eventually killed him."* A reliable source close to Michael told me.

Martin Bashir's documentary could be described some sort of a *'written obituary'* of Michael Jackson. Because of it, some people till this day still see Michael Jackson as a man who lived with underage children and sexually molested them. Bashir's *Living with Michael Jackson* has since been described by some people as an opinionated piece of journalism which was masqueraded as a documentary. Knowing fully well that Michael Jackson was a global brand, Martin Bashir was aware of what he would achieve by making a documentary about him. Michael Jackson knew his own worth as well and that was one of the reasons he mostly refused to give access to many journalists to interview him as he suspected they might exploit his name and image to make money and raise their profile. However, with Martin Bashir, he badly miscalculated and paid the price for it.

Bashir and his sponsors chased Michael for two years before the King of Pop eventually caved in and accepted their proposal to do a documentary about him. Bashir's documentary made lot of money for the ITV in England which sponsored it as well as for the co-producer who was Martin Bashir. Indeed, after the documentary was aired in Britain, ABC was reported to have snapped the rights to broadcast it in America for $5 million dollars, besides hiring Bashir as an anchor in the States afterwards. *New York Times* later described the documentary as *"callous self-interest masked as sympathy"*. Dieter Wiesner, Jackson's personal manager from 1996-2003, said of Bashir's documentary after Michael's death: *"It broke him. It killed him. He took a long time to die but it started that night. Previously the drugs were a crutch but after that documentary, they became a necessity."* While Michael was destroyed, the Pakistani-British journalist who made the controversial documentary became the toast of America's white-controlled media. It was reported at the time that ABC and NBC fell over each other to hire

Martin Bashir as an anchor until he finally settled at ABC.

When he was alive, still reeling from the damage the documentary caused him Michael released a statement which was too little, too late, saying of Martin Bashir: *"I trusted him to come into my life and that of my family. He told me that he was the man that turned Diana's life around. I am surprised that a professional journalist would compromise his integrity by deceiving me in this way. I feel more betrayed than perhaps ever before; that someone, who had got to know my children, my staff and me, whom I let into my heart and told the truth, could then sacrifice the trust I placed in him and produce this terrible and unfair programme. Everyone who knows me will know the truth which is that my children come first in my life and that I would never harm any child. I also want to thank my fans around the world for the overwhelming number of messages of support that I have received, particularly from Great Britain, where people have emailed me and said how appalled they were by Bashir's documentary. Their love and support has touched me greatly."*

Two days after the death of Michael Jackson, Bashir appeared on his ABC TV show to praise him as a legend and an icon. What cheek of a man!

CHAPTER TEN

THE DAMAGE OF LATOYA JACKSON

"Michael is my brother and I love him a great deal, but I cannot and will not be a silent collaborator of his crimes against small children"

-La Toya Jackson

After the break up of Jackson 5 in the early 1980s, Michael and his brothers moved out of the Jackson family mansion called *Hayvenhurst* in the suburb of Encino California to set up their respective homes in different parts of California. When the Jackson brothers went their separate ways, they still felt like a solid and unbreakable family and hoped that they would continue to maintain contact with each other and from time to time get together at *Hayvenhurst* for family reunion. Michael was the last of the Jackson 5 to leave *Hayvenhurst* and move to his opulent *Neverland* ranch home in the Santa Ynez valley of California in 1990. About this time after the huge success of *Thriller*, he was also heavily involved with some of the other albums that would later make him one of the greatest musicians ever. According to my sources, at that time, he wanted some peace and private time which he needed to complete the music projects he had in mind and therefore had no choice but to reduce, if not completely cut off communication with his family.

Meanwhile, her sister LaToya who had been flirting with show business at the time had also left the family home *Hayvenhurst,* dumped her father who was managing her start-up music career at the time and went off with a new manager called Jack Gordon. LaToya went travelling the world with her new manager to promote her fledging music career. Although the Jackson brothers had each set up homes in different parts of California, however, once in a while, they would gather at *Hayvenhurst* with their respective families to celebrate one event or the other.

One of the most important family get-togethers in those days was the celebration of their mother's birthday. Michael loved his mother and inspite of his busy schedule with some new music project, would find time to attend his mother's birthday party. As Michael was also the wealthiest of the brothers, he was the one who mostly funded Katherine's birthday bash. When some of the family reunion took place in those days, LaToya was mostly absent because she was away from America with Jack Gordon as she was promoting her music career around the world. Invariably with her continued absence from America, the gulf between her and the family grew. It is also said that Jack Gordon played a vital role in making LaToya alienate herself from the Jackson family.

Michael was very close to his mother Katherine and extended the same closeness to sisters Rebbie and Janet. Although Michael had a third sister, LaToya, he rarely confided in her as he had reservations about her. This was not to say that Michael did not love his sister LaToya, he did very much but for some reason as highlighted in the latter part of this chapter, did not get along with her as much as he did with the other women in his family. For example, when Michael secretly married Lisa Marie Presley in the Bahamas, he called their mother and other sisters to inform them, but not LaToya. So why didn't Michael get on well with LaToya? Well through my research for this book, I gathered that when she and her brothers were growing up back in Gary, Indiana in the 1960s, LaToya was seen as a petulant girl by her siblings. Even at their young age in those days, her brothers would do their best to avoid her because she always wanted to land them in trouble by reporting to their parents that the boys were naughty and fighting with each other when their parents were out. Although she was shy and quiet, she was the type of person one could describe as a 'green snake in a green grass'. I was told by sources close to the Jackson family at the time that LaToya constantly seeked attention and favour from their parents. She always wanted to give the impression that she was the good one and her siblings the bad ones. My source told me: *"La Toya would be the first to run to Katherine and Joseph to report that her brothers have been fighting or misbehaving while they were out.While she would have sworn allegiance to her brothers not to tell their parents, she would often break such allegiance the moment their parents stepped into the house and report that the boys have been fighting. Sometimes, it didn't matter if she had to make up some stuff, all La Toya was after was for the Jacksons' parents to see her as the good one"*

Being also self-centred, at school LaToya would go out of her way to find kids who would like to be friends with her because she is LaToya and not because of her family connection to Jackson 5. LaToya's resentment of her brothers' string of successes when they were in Jackson 5 and later of Michael when he went solo did not start when they have grown up but it was a deep-rooted resentment which actually started as far back as when she was a young girl growing up with her siblings in Gary Indiana. In spite of the fact that the success of Jackson 5 provided the family with wealth and influence from which LaToya herself benefitted, she saw her brothers' successes as a burden which she imagined would negatively impact her own music career. Although LaToya is probably the least talented of the Jackson siblings, she did release some albums of her own over the years with Michael featuring in one of them. But the result of all her efforts in music could never be compared or match the string of successes of Jackson 5 including that of her superstar brother Michael or infact younger sister Janet who came on the scene later. As LaToya found her siblings' respective successes hard to accept, she decided that she had to gain her own publicity too. And to her, it didn't matter how she went about it.

After moving out of the family home at about the age of 30, LaToya embarked on a solo career in music and with a manager who could best be described as a crook, set about seeking success and publicity for her self. Her opportunity came when Michael was accused of molesting Jody Chandler in 1993. As Michael was in America fighting the case, LaToya surprised her family by popping up on TV in Israel to denounce her brother. According to her, sleeping with teenage boys was something which Michael had been doing from as far back as when they all lived together at *Hayvenhurst* their family home in Encino California. She said she came on TV to inform the world of what had been going on from a long time before Jody Chandler and that she was duty bound to condemn her brother's behavior. She also said that their parents knew about Michael's interest in young boys from that time but kept quiet because Michael was the bread winner of the family and that their parents did not want to upset him. She told viewers: *"Michael is my brother and I love him a great deal, but I cannot and will not be a silent collaborator of his crimes against small children."* Then she followed up her rant the next day in an NBC interview claiming that their mother had once referred to Michael as *"a damn faggot"*. But LaToya was not finished yet; with the intention of getting more publicity, she also humiliated her family further by claiming that her father also abused her when she lived at home and that their mother was a collaborator as well because she kept quiet and let her father did what he did to her. With her name now in the public eye, her aim and wishes to become famous was fulfilled as on her return to America from Israel in 1994, she was approached once again by *Playboy* to pose for the third time in their men's magazine and publicity video. LaToya against her family's wishes had initially posed for *Playboy* in 1989 and 1991. With her 3rd appearance in *Playboy* this time more raunchy, LaToya who was raised with the Jehova Witness Faith infuriated her family further which led to her self-imposed exile from the family. But that did not bother LaToya as she went on to also host a soft porn variety show on national TV.

According to my sources, LaToya's outbursts against

her brother during the Jody Chandler sexual accusation broke Michael's heart and caused him to cry for many days and nights. He could not understand how his sister would go on TV to condemn him and say the things she said about him and young boys. According to my source *"Michael was so upset with his sister that he swore never to talk to her again until the day he dies."* However, some years after LaToya returned back to her family from Jack Gordon, their mother Katherine called for a peace talk between Michael and LaToya. Michael loved his mother Katherine and would never disobey her. So the two siblings met at the family's home and made up. It took 10 years to bring brother and sister together but irrespective of the peace deal, it was an open secret that Michael and LaToya's renewed relationship, which was never the strongest anyway, became more of a show to please their mother than genuine brother–sister relationship.

Meanwhile, since Michael passed away in 2009, LaToya has been going on TV and radio channels to give interviews which suggest some kind of conspiracy for the death of her brother. While talking about her brother's death, she has also been blaming other people for her failings and missteps in the past. Watching the clips of her interviews today, what resonates in me was that damaging statement she made against her brother and family in Israel in 1993. LaToya was a grown woman at the time she was running her brother and family down; she probably was in her 30s, so she cannot now pretend or claim that she did not know what she was doing then. It leaves much to be desired for her to be going around to tell the world that her ex-husband forced her to go on TV and annihilate her brother and family in equal measure. LaToya was very much aware that she was using her brother's 1993 scandal to seek publicity for herself. After upsetting her family in the 1990s, she is now going around TV and radio stations to spin tales which depicts her as a victim whilst taking no responsibility for her actions in the past. She blames all her poor decisions and actions in those days on her ex-husband

Jack Gordon who may have been a shady character, but it is also difficult to believe that LaToya was as naive and innocent as she claims to be especially, when considering that she posed for *Playboy* not once but three times. In order to promote her appearances in the magazine and increase publicity for herself, she decided that the best way to do it at that time was to run her family down in the most vicious way possible. LaToya was raised in a musical family that were also very much into the entertainment business. One believes also that she was very much aware of what is involved in appearing in mens' magazine. For her to appear in *Playboy* on three occasion, who signed the model release and who received the fees? LaToya might have been in an abusive relationship with Jack Gordon but the extent to which she pratically abdicated her responsibility as an adult is what I find difficult to comprehend. About the time LaToya was denouncing her family on television and in newspapers, Janet Jackson, her sister, was interviewed and asked why her elder sister was humiliating the family. Janet hinted that her sister might have been jealous of her sibling's success and was lashing back in frustration and or possibly to seek her own publicity too.

So while LaToya implied disdain for Michael when he was alive, she has been going around since his death to profess her love for him. She has also been in the forefront to find out who might have murdered her brother. Michael may have forgiven his sister before he passed but I have been told that the relationship between them was at best formal in order to keep their mother happy.

Reliable sources close to Michael told me: *"Most of the things LaToya has been saying about Michael since he passed away are exaggerated and fabricated. Her conspiratory theories regarding Michael's death do not make sense. She was not in Michael's life as she is now implying and did not know anything about his business dealings either. When everyone abandoned Michael, it was I and a few of my colleagues who stayed with him. And inspite of the fact that there were difficulties getting our wages, we were the ones who were there for him until his final days. What LaToya is saying about her brother's death are stuff based on what she might have read in the newspapers. If she knows who planned or was involved in the murder of her brother why not name them?"*

While this book discusses the damage done to Michael Jackson by the media, the establishment and gold diggers, one cannot ignore the role played by his sister LaToya in destroying him too. LaToya's resentment and jealousy of her brother's success got the best of her and blindly led her to contribute with others to gravely damage him. *"Michael might have reconciled with LaToya before his death but he did so in order to placate their mother who demanded family unity from time to time. But in his heart, he never forgave LaToya for betraying him when he was in trouble. Drugs might have played a part but truth is Michael died of heartbreak caused by all the troubles he faced in the latter part of his life. He died a very unhappy man."* My sources concluded.

CHAPTER ELEVEN
PAEDOPHILE OR MISUNDERSTOOD

"It didn't matter if he was proven innocent or otherwise. He carried the burden with him until his final breath"

- *Michael Jackson's staff*

Michael Jackson did not help himself as he kept forming close friendship with teenage boys. He had problems about his association with young boys in 1993 and again in 2003. Irrespective of the above, the conclusion I came to in the course of researching this book was that he befriended young boys because he wanted to reclaim the childhood he felt he lost when he joined the family band, Jackson 5 at the young age of 5. Michael missed out on childrens' stuff like kicking around baseball, basketball or simply playing and running around in public parks with other children. He also missed out on such things as pillow fighting, story telling and watching cartoons on TV. Many of these children's hobbies passed Michael by as he was fully engaged in rehearsing, producing records in the studio and touring with his brothers from1960s to mid1980s. From when he was 5 years old to adolescent, he never had the opportunity to play with people of his age outside his brothers and sisters all of whom before Randy and Janet were born were older than him. So when he became an adult and had moved to his own home he thought of bringing back his childhood by befriending teenagers who visited his opulent home *Neverland* from time to time and spend the day playing with them.This might not seem right in the eyes of many of us but he did not see anything wrong with his choice of teenage friends. Infact he built *Neverland* for the sole purpose of entertaining himself and his young friends. The question is, was his association with the teenagers sexual? I am assured by those closest to him who spoke to me that that was not the case. Whatever, he was never found guilty of any inappropriate behaviour with young boys. In the course of my research, I never came across any evidence of child molestation by Michael either through documents, images, videos or any hint of that from people who worked for him and spoke to me on condition of anonymity. Irrespective of the above however, what was certain was that the two alleged child abuse allegations which he successfully fought in 1993 and again in 2003-4 took their toll on his health and finances, damaged his personality and stalled his music career. He paid $200 million to quash the first allegation in 1993 and the court acquitted him of the second allegation in 2004. Meanwhile, Evan Chandler 65, father of Jody Chandler who instigated the first allegation in 1993 and demanded the ransom of $200 million which Michael Jackson paid, committed suicide on 17th November 2009 just five months after Michael Jackson passed away. Could it be that nemesis caught up with Evan Chandler? It is up to you reading this book have to draw your own conclusion.

Beside Jackson's acquittal in 2004 as regards the case of Garvin Avizo, further investigations were carried out in America by the FBI and CIA. Secret agents from the two agencies flew to the Philippines to interview key witnesses who are a couple called Mark and Faye Quindoy. The couple worked as domestic staff for Michael Jackson at his *Neverland* mansion between the 1980s and 1990s. But before the interviews with FBI and CIA agents, the couple had passed on their story to some tabloids in England in which they claimed that they saw some inappropriate things happen between Michael Jackson and teenage boys at *Neverland*. I was reliably informed by fellow staff members who worked together with the Quindoys at *Neverland* at the time that *"the Quindoys were relieved of their job by Michael long before the Jody Chandler case. But when they realised that he was in trouble they thought of a revenge and concocted a story which they passed on to the tabloids''*. But their story did not stack up with the FBI and the CIA and were dismissed by the agencies.

In England, the American secret service agents also looked into the allegation of a certain Terry George who made a bogus claim in the *The Sun* that Michael Jackson sexually assaulted him when he was a teenager. Terry George claimed that Michael engaged him in regular phone sex, calling him all the way from America at nights to engage in phone sex with him when he was 13 years old. He also claimed that he and Michael had a physical sexual encounter when the latter was in London to perform sometime in the 1980s. *The Sun* as expected, was excited by Terry's claim and spent days running the news on their pages. But it was later discovered that Terry George was a man who owned a series of phone-sex agencies and was of questionable character. It also emerged that the only contact Terry George ever had with Michael Jackson was when the singer obliged for a photo request by Terry George back stage during one of Michael's live concerts in London. It was that photo in which Michael appeared with George that the latter used to convince opportunistic tabloids that he was well known to Michael Jackson and therefore had a sexual relationship with him. As always with any news concerning Michael Jackson, the English tabloids blew the story out of proportion and ran it many times in order to increase newspaper sales.

The American agencies-FBI and CIA after carrying out their investigations in America, Australia, England and the Philippines, ruled that *"NO EVIDENCE EXISTED TO PROVE THAT MICHAEL JACKSON WAS ENGAGED IN CHILD ABUSE IN AMERICA, OR IN ANY OTHER COUNTRY."* They dismissed the Quindoys and Terry George's allegations as inadmissible. However, the English tabloids ignored the findings of the FBI and the CIA and continued to serialize sex abuse stories against Michael Jackson, most of which were unfounded. It is not difficult to see why the tabloids decided to ignore the FBI and CIA findings-it was in their financial interest to continue to publish sensational stories about Michael Jackson so that they could increase circulation of their newspapers.While tabloids profited from publishing lies about Michael Jackson, the singer's reputation was destroyed forever.

It is obvious till this day that not everyone was happy about Michael Jackson's success irrespective of how much they pretended to love him. The American establishment and the white media in America and Britain which have been unable to bring him down at the height of his opulence, bided their time until the child abuse allegations presented them with a golden opportunity to deal with him.They know very well that once an allegation of child abuse is made against somebody and if that person is a megastar as Michael Jackson was, it wouldn't matter if he is not found guilty by the court, the damage was already done. In the media's quest for exclusivity about child sex abuse story, Sir Cliff Richard, one of Britain's top singers from the 1960s was damaged by the BBC some years ago and although the police in England have cleared him of any wrong doing, he feels aggrieved because he knows that the BBC has caused him irreparable damage. Michael Jackson might have been a mega star but he was also the victim of a systematic racial profiling and bullying from America to Britain.

Evaluating all the information I have gathered from reliable sources while researching this book, it may not be an overstatement to say that in addition to the effects of Propofol and Demerol, Micheal Jackson died of heart attack as a result of all the troubles he was facing and which he saw no end in sight. The problems he encountered when he was alive and which came from all angles depressed him very much and led him to begin to use powerful anti depressant drugs which eventually killed him. Michael Jackson's life was a mixture of success, eccentricity, depression, frustration and bad luck.

He missed out on his childhood, got heavily burnt in 1984, got entangled with child abuse allegations not once but twice and was pursued by gold diggers and the media. It is sad to say that Michael was a troubled guy. By the time he was in his mid-forties leading up to his death at 51 years, he was already a broken man. Prophetically, 20 years earlier, he had said that he didn't think he *'would ever be totally a happy person'*. From the age of 20 or so when he left his family home at Encino, California to live on his own, he had no one from his protective family to guide him, instead he surrounded himself with sycophants, then degenerated into drug addiction and the rest is now history. Jackson's life and his incredible talent raise the possibility of a myth about him. It is difficult to decipher whether Michael Jackson was some kind of divine miracle-part human and part spirit. *"No one knows what or who I am. No one knows the truth. And the longer it takes to know, to discover this, the more famous I will be"*, he wrote in his *Moonwalk* book of 1988.

In music and sports: Elvis Presley, The Beatles, Rolling Stones, Bob Marley, Pink Floyd, Tupac Shakur, Fela Anikulapo Kuti, Mohammed Ali, Pele, Maradona, Messi, Ronaldo, Tiger Woods and others might have brought about a new style of living but Michael Jackson's contribution and influence in our world eclipses every thing the others might have achieved. On his death on 25 June 2009, Al Shampton, the American civil rights leader said this of him: *"Michael Jackson made the rest of the world accept a person of colour way before Tiger Woods, way before Oprah Winfrey and way before Barack Obama. Michael Jackson was a trailblazer!"*

CHAPTER TWELVE

THIS IS IT! –*Fall of an icon*

"This is it, this really is it," Michael Jackson triumphantly announced in his last official public appearance at the O2 Arena in London on March 5, 2009. If only he had any idea how prophetic that phrase would turn out to be because the King of Pop was dead before his triumphant comeback. Michael Jackson's death was the final bizarre twist in music's strangest soap opera. His life and the circumstances of his death could also be viewed as music comedy vs real life drama, played out in public, the media and court inquisitions.

Michael Jackson was a child star who rose to become the greatest pop icon of our time. Although raised as a Jehovah Witness, his music and lifestyle did not conform to the religious doctrine he and his family professed. His astronomic success and the exploitation of the wealth he made through music by people from different walks of life brought him lot of pain. As his troubles multiplied the world saw Michael Jackson crumble away slowly until he tragically passed on 25 June 2009. At the time of his death, there were about 33 law suits against him, majority of which were by people who hardly know him personally but wanted to gain something from him. During his life time he paid out more than $400 million dollars in litigation, most of which also went to people who didn't know much about him apart from his music. He thought that the best way to get people off his back and leave him alone was by paying out huge ransoms and after that lock up himself in his mansion. Then he became a virtual recluse.

He lost huge amount of money, if not all of the money he had made in a career that spanned more than 40 years. He mutilated his appearance in a vain attempt to turn himself into his childhood hero, Peter Pan. He got involved in friendship with young boys and became the man who never grew up. His last well known home *Neverland* hidden in the Santa Ynez Valley of California, became the seat of his empire housing monkeys, chimps, snakes and other animals he kept for company. *Neverland* also served as a venue where he hosted his teenage friends. He married and divorced Elvis Presley's daughter and went on to acquire children through surrogate mothers, none of whom is said seem to carry his genes.

The truth is that most of the decisions Michael took in life were perplexing if not lacking in good judgment.The media might have been hard on him but the eccentricity he exhibited served also as the perfect recipe for the media's intrusion in his life.

Michael Jackson suffered constant harassment and ruthless speculation from the media which carried on until the day he died and continued afterwards because the world media still continued to publish sensational stories about him until he was finally laid to rest. While some private individuals and organizations were jealous of his success and did not seem to accept him, others decided to cash in and exploit him. Now that he is gone, may be the world would leave him alone!

"This is it, this really is it,"-**Michael Jackson**

The Michael Jackson phenomenon which caught our attention from when he was a child star and captivated us through to his adulthood linked people regardless of class, race and geography. Unfortunately his legacy also created a superstar which many of us did not quite understand. The strange behaviours he exhibited divided peoples' opinion; so much so that by the time he died in 2009 the American nation, presided over by the first black President, Barack Obama was already negatively influenced by the gutter press and sensational stories which made Obama to ignore his death and funeral service. Some people say that the bad press Michael received, especially towards the later part of his life, was one of the reasons Obama decided to deny him a national burial.The President bowing to pressure from the Washington establishment and their white media and possibly wrestling also with his own fear that Michael Jackson was a better known black man than himself, took the decision to ignore his death. President Obama did not make any statement about Michael Jackson's death until after 24 hours had passed. And when the President spoke about Michael Jackson's death, he only made a half-hearted statement which was actually prompted by a foreign journalist who confronted him about it.

Michael Jackson died 8 years ago and as the dust has settled down what exactly are we to make of him and his life? How should we remember the King of Pop? The answer, me thinks would depend on how each one of us view him.Whatever, one thing no one can take away from him is that he broke cultural taboos across the world with his music and left us in awe of his incredible talent which we all witnessed from when he was a precocious child of 5 years old. In his music career which spanned 45 years, Michael Jackson released 68 singles, 10 solo studio albums, one live album, 64 compilation albums and 4 remix albums. *Thriller,* his 6th album which was released in 1982 remains to this day, the world's best-selling album.

Finally, irrespective of the turbulence and turmoil he went through, Michael Jackson lived a life of generosity, humility and love. In those days, as I have been reliably informed by people that were close to him, out of the glare of the media, Michael Jackson would often open the gates of his home *Neverland* and let in hungry people to dine, walk around and play with him in his compound. The visiting children and their parents would enjoy the fun parks that surrounded the ranch and later be sent home with presents. Although his life turned out to become a drama which was played out in full public view, Michael Jackson lived a life in which he gave back to the world as much as he got from it.

FURTHER ACKNOWLEDGEMENTS AND REFERENCE SOURCES

Below is a list of other sources the author consulted in the preparation and writing of this book of which he is immensely grateful:

MOONWALK by Michael Jackson published by Mandarin, London, 1992

YOU ARE NOT ALONE MICHAEL: THROUGH A BROTHER'S EYE by Jermaine Jackson, published by HarperCollins, London, 2011

MICHAEL JACKSON: THE LIFE OF AN ICON (DVD) by David Gest

THE WASHINGTON POST

NEW YORK TIMES

DAILY MAIL (England)

MAIL ON SUNDAY (England)

NEWS OF THE WORLD (England)

THE SUN ON SUNDAY (England)

THE SUN (England)

DAILY STAR (England)

DAILY MIRROR (England)